Matchmaking
From Fun to Profit

Also from the Matchmaking Institute:

Make Me a Match
The 21ˢᵗ Century Guide to Finding and Using a Matchmaker

Matchmaking
From Fun to Profit

A Complete Guide to Turning
Your Matchmaking Skills
into a New Business

Matchmaking Institute[SM]

Introduction by Lisa Clampitt, CSW
Contributors:
Lisa Clampitt, Jerome Chasques,
Jill Weaver, Rob Anderson, and Steven Sacks

Skyhorse Publishing

Library of Congress Cataloging-in-Publication Data

Matchmaking from fun to profit : a complete guide to turning your matchmaking skills into a new business / Matchmaking Institute ; Lisa Clampitt ... [et al.].
    p. cm.
 Includes bibliographical references.
  ISBN 978-1-60239-110-9 (pbk. : alk. paper)
 1. New business enterprises. 2. Dating services. 3. Mate selection. I. Clampitt, Lisa. II. Matchmaking Institute.

HD62.5.M358 2007
392.6—dc22

                        2007020061

Interior design by Elise Smith
Printed in the United States of America

And, in the end,
the love you take is equal to
the love you make.

—*The Beatles*

Contents

Introduction

Dear Reader,

I have a fun, rewarding, and enjoyable job. I make my own hours, I go out most nights, and generally have a great time. I only work with people I like, and I never take on ethically compromising assignments. However, strangely enough, I have few peers in my field. As such, there is very little common knowledge surrounding my business, and public perception tends to be rampant with stereotypes, misinformation, and misconceptions. That's why I wanted to write this book with my fellow colleagues from the Matchmaking Institute and set the record straight about an industry that has historically been shrouded in mystery and stigma: matchmaking.

That's right. I'm a matchmaker. I've been an old-fashioned, face-to-face matchmaker for the past eight years and I love it. Before pursuing a career in professional matchmaking, I worked with people in a very different arena: I was a social worker. During my twelve years in social work, including a three-year tenure at Bellevue Hospital in New York, I worked primarily with children and families under extreme emotional duress. Naturally, the job began to take its toll on me, and I found myself more and more emotionally drained, and less and less professionally effectual in my position. I wanted to continue working with people in a supportive, helping capacity, but was having an increasingly difficult time handling these very sensitive cases. So, I turned my love of counseling, working with people, and helping others into something more upbeat: a career as a professional matchmaker.

So welcome to *Matchmaking From Fun to Profit*, an in-depth look at an age-old profession, and a guide for keeping the traditions of matchmaking alive.

Over the last ten years, the career of matchmaking has made a huge comeback and now, more than ever, singles are enlisting professional matchmakers to help them find love. The continued and exponential growth in the matchmaking industry demonstrates that today's singles are putting their love life at the top of their priority list. There has never been a better time to enter the field of matchmaking!

This guide will not only provide you with the information necessary to create the perfect match, it will also explain the many nuances of matchmaking in the twenty-first century. From choosing your first client to harnessing your personal market value, this book will give you the skills you need to start your very own matchmaking business.

Matchmaking is an excellent way to become self-employed in a business that is yours to name and profit from as you see fit. But more importantly, it will give the opportunity to cultivate the most sacred emotion that we, as human beings, so greatly prize and cherish: love.

Lisa Clampitt, CSW
Professional Matchmaker
Matchmaking Institute Executive Director

PART I

The Field of Matchmaking

In the Beginning . . .

1

Matchmakers, arranged marriages, child brides—these sound like terms from medieval times. Certainly throughout most of history, marriage was not considered a matter of the heart. Instead, marriage was treated as a business deal arranged and negotiated with financial gain, societal status, and/or family lineage in mind. First came marriage, then (hopefully) came love. Communities relied on experts to pair up their young: the wise, well-respected *nokado* in Japan, the *portador* in Mexico, the *kalyn* in Russia. Certainly, we all remember the colorful Yenta in Joseph Stein's Broadway play, *Fiddler on the Roof.* Whether she was real or fabricated is not certain. But we do know that in many cultures the role of matchmaker is akin to that of a spiritual advisor. For example, matchmaking was considered a function (albeit a peripheral one) of the village priest in medieval Catholic society. Similarly, in Orthodox Jewish communities, the shadchan takes his role of setting people up for marriage quite seriously. He researches and makes inquiries into prospective partners (their character, financial status, family background, degree of religious observance) and serves as an emotional boundary keeper at the beginning stages of the dating ritual. He often helps iron out problems or when necessary informs the family that a match is not going to work.

For centuries, a matchmaker served as the facilitator for what in essence was a business transaction of the highest magnitude. The union that ensued, at times among partners who had never set eyes on one another, was a pragmatic one meant to concentrate power and wealth, consolidate properties, and secure lineages. It was the ultimate diplomatic tool. Arranged marriages were especially important in dowry-based inheritance systems, where women only inherited male wealth at the time of marriage, making parents particularly attentive to their daughters' matches. Even today, wealthy European merchant families continue to marry into impoverished noble families in order to obtain a coveted title.

In America, during the mid-1800s, mail-order brides became popular among pioneers heading west to settle on the open, untamed land. These men needed hardy women willing to work hard. So, they advertised in newspapers to find wives who would brave the harsh conditions. And today, with the advent of the Internet, mail-order bride sites are proliferating, offering women from Russia, the Ukraine, Kazakhstan, Uzbekistan, the Philippines, Thailand, and many other less privileged countries.

Likewise, in almost forty African and Middle Eastern countries, a go-between such as a family member or town elder arranges marriages for underage females. In India, China, and Japan, a significant number of marriages continue to be arranged by family members. You probably won't have these types of clients as a professional matchmaker in the United States, but it is important to be aware of the different cultures and histories some of your clients may come from. It's especially fascinating to note that while India has perhaps the most arranged marriages, it also reputedly has one of the lowest divorce rates of any country in the world. This certainly suggests that the individual touch of matchmatching helps create stronger, more lasting relationships.

"Today the matchmaker is viewed as more of a professional headhunter for the heart than as a meddling yenta," says Lisa Clampitt.

In America, love is viewed as an inalienable right. Finding a life partner is added to people's "to-do" list along with paying the credit card bill and booking that much needed Caribbean vacation. Americans can be as discriminating about their love choice as they are about finding the right apartment, job, or pair of shoes. So, rather than wait patiently for Mr. or Mrs. Right to arrive, people are searching for love where they search for everything else—online. Online dating started with America Online in the early 1990s. In 1995 Match.com took the helm with numerous others trailing in its wake: JDate, Yahoo! Personals, eHarmony, Lavalife, and more. While statistics show that many people enjoy surfing the Net for a date, the success ratios remain unclear. And while online dating sites have become great at targeting specific niche markets, i.e., religions, careers, hobbies, etc., there are many complaints about authenticity and safety. In fact, reports abound of made-up profiles, false or out-of-date photos, and lies people have no problem telling. Many people miss the personal aspect of "old-fashioned" dating. So in a way, the obsession with online dating has spawned an obsession with the more current concept of offline dating.

Today, instead of being introduced by the village elder, unmarried men and women attend singles events, go on dating game shows, participate in reality television shows, and take part in speed dating. Yet, the most effective of all offline dating options is matchmaking. Why? Because people value the personal touch and want the sense of community a matchmaker can bring into their lives. It's no accident that matchmaking is a $236 million business (part of the $1.08 billion total for the dating industry in 2006). After all, it's been in existence in one form or another for thousands of years. Welcome to the growing, challenging, and enriching field of matchmaking.

The Ins and Outs
of Matchmaking

2

Executive Director and cofounder of the Matchmaking Institute™, Lisa Clampitt, spent years pairing her friends together for fun before deciding upon matchmaking as a career. Lisa was formerly a social worker, connecting people in need with the appropriate services to help them. Lisa found great joy in helping others, but there were far too many unhappy endings. Lisa wanted to find a job where she could use her social work skills as a means to a higher level of satisfaction—both for her clients and herself.

Lisa made the transformation from social worker to matchmaker by creating a personal coaching program at an already-established matchmaking company. Via this company, she began to receive press as a "relationship expert," and after only two years, realized she could easily start her very own matchmaking service.

Lisa quickly discovered that when it came to finding love, money was no object. Human beings will sacrifice almost anything for love because love means happiness—and we all want to be happy.

Getting to Know Your Client

As a matchmaker, you will be selling a highly desired product. The challenge will be finding clients confident enough to seek the help you are offering. Despite the plethora of self-help books on the market—dieting, spirituality, moneymaking, self-empowerment, etc.—people

> Always remember,
> you are a matchmaker,
> NOT a therapist.

have a hard time seeking help when it comes to relationships. It's as if society wants us to believe that love is a personal issue to be handled on our own. Lisa knows otherwise and urges her clients to approach finding a mate as they would approach finding a job—without shame and proactively. This includes seeking all the help you can find.

Lisa says "The sad thing about it is that a lot of times, people think, 'God, I'm a loser if I'm single.' They say to themselves, 'If I say I need help, that means I'm a even more of a loser . . . so, I like being single.' Some people feel healthy and great being single, but the majority want to find someone . . . and I feel passionately that most people would benefit from having a matchmaker in their lives to help them succeed in finding a satisfying relationship."

It will be your job to encourage clients to open up and help them learn more about themselves in order to discover who their best match will be. By working with you, singles will be given the opportunity to date safely. Clients will be screened by you before ever meeting their potential match. This enables you to pair the people whose wants and needs are most compatible. As a matchmaker, you not only gain satisfaction upon cultivating the perfect match, but during the dating process you will watch your clients learn and grow, eventually making better decisions for themselves.

Lisa learned early on that it is important to encourage your client to examine *why* he or she is single. Ask them if they feel that they have been proactive in their search. In what ways? What is their "type"?

Lisa recalls a woman stating that she goes out all the time and there are just no good men out there. When further questions were asked, it became clear that every time she went out she went with a group of women, which made it virtually impossible for her to be approached by a man. She then indicated that when she is out with her friends she does not like it when men approach her.

It is your job to help clients discover what hasn't worked in the past so that together you can agree on resolutions for the future. Lisa explains, "The reality is, even the most self-aware people can use some introspection on who they are and who they choose."

> *Encourage your client's proactive behavior:* There is no downside to being friendly. It is important for both men and women to be emotionally available and APPROACHABLE! Encourage them to smile, say "Good Morning." What can it hurt?!

Find out about your clients' dating patterns

Lisa also emphasizes the importance of noticing patterns. For example: Does your client always date the "bad guy"? Or, does your client always date the "model-type"? Why are they doing this and what are they really looking for in a date? Encourage your clients to set high standards for themselves and reassure them that if they are truly open to finding someone, they will!

However, do be aware of those clients with the never-ending shopping list of requirements: He must be at least six feet tall but under six feet two inches, have an athletic build but not too much muscle, make over two hundred thousand a year, have all of his hair, hold a graduate degree from an Ivy League school, be social, drive a high-end car, have his own friends, be a good cook, wear designer shoes, etc. It is most often the clients with the longest lists who carry the most personal insecurities. It is then your job to turn it back on them, to ask them if they're looking for love or if they're building a firewall. Which of these requirements are acting as cover-ups for their own insecurities?

Everyone has a story from their previous relationships. Ask your client's for theirs: Was it love at first sight? Were they friends first? Did opposites attract? What did their ex look like? How and why did it end?

Then ask them about their dating habits: How are they on a date? Do they tend to talk about themselves the entire time? Are they able to reciprocate and listen? Do they drink too much on the first date? Do they generally sleep with someone on the first date?

Gathering as much information about your client and maintaining an open and honest policy is imperative to your ability as a matchmaker. The more you understand about your client's dating record, the better you will be at providing improvement.

Choosing your clientele

Most people who seek your services will be looking for serious relationships. There will be those few, however, that are simply looking to pass the time. They aren't serious about finding Mr. or Mrs. Right, but they are interested in using your services for entertainment purposes.

Lisa firmly believes that matchmaking is very much about your personal values, and the ways in which you feel you can (and want) to help someone. So, ethically, you have to decide if you feel comfortable taking on a client who is looking to pass the time and wants social fill-in rather than a long-term relationship. Whomever you decide to work with, you must clearly communicate your clients' relationship goals to their matches and match them accordingly.

As a general rule, before taking on any client it is wise to decipher whether it makes sense for you to work with this person. Ask yourself: Will I be able to get along with this person? Will they value my services? Does this person make me feel comfortable? Is this person open to change? Will this person work with me or against me? Would they be an asset or liability to my company?

Upon meeting potential clients, think about placing them, much like a staffing industry would place a hopeful candidate. Do you already have their match-type in your database? Are their requests reasonable? How much time would you estimate you'll have to spend matching them? What do they have going for them? Will they be an easy sell to potential matches?

Being at the top of your game—advising and coaching

Make sure you know what's out there. The world of dating is constantly changing; new rules apply, old traditions change, expectations fluctuate. As a matchmaker, people will look to you for advice; you will become an automatic authority on dating, relationships, and love. Make sure that you can provide dating tips, fashion advice, and etiquette training when necessary.

This means educating yourself in the ways of dating, relationships, and love. For example: *He's Just Not That Into You*—you've read it. *Dating for Dummies*—you could have written it. *Hitch*—seen it.

Many people that come to you will need help in all areas of dating—finding a date will only be half of what they will need. Lisa suggests that it might behoove both your clientele and your business to offer a personal coaching/image consulting package in addition to your matchmaking services.

"You may call it personal coaching, image coaching, or even wardrobe consulting, and cover everything from first-date tactics to hairstyling. Some matchmakers even provide references to cosmetic dentists and plastic surgeons. This type of package is for someone who may not have a clue, and this is your way of holding his or her hand, saying, 'Whatever you need, I can provide.'"

Matchmaking as a Business

Before dealing with the how-to's of matchmaking, there are a few key ingredients that mustn't be overlooked.

Niche market

Ask yourself

- Have you chosen a particular niche market?
- Have you decided upon an appropriate price structure?
- Do you have an idea for your business model?
- How do you plan on building/maintaining your database of clientele?

Let's start with finding a niche. Choosing a specific niche allows you to maintain a focus within your database of clientele. It also serves to attract a more like-minded group of singles, making it easier for you to match, and for them to choose. For example, if a woman has a specific financial requirement, why would she go to Match.com, when she could seek your services knowing that, you as a matchmaker prequalify the information you are given, so that her number one requirement is already satisfied?

Age groups are an excellent way to narrow your business and still maintain an open market. There are also those matchmakers who enjoy paring singles based upon their hobbies, professions, even their nonprofit interests! When choosing a niche, it is important to consider your working area. Are you near a predominantly gay, retired, or young community? Do you prefer working with only female clients? Are you trying to appeal to a certain paying class? Asking yourself these questions will help you determine the ease in which you can create a client base.

Price structure

When deciding upon a price structure for your new business, you will have to determine both the advantages and disadvantages of your surrounding geography and demographics. Generally speaking, if you live in a smaller town, you probably won't be charging as much as you will if you are living in a larger city such as New York, Los Angeles, or Miami. Research your community to figure out what other services you will be competing with, and with whom you'll most likely be working: How many singles are in your area? What are their ages? (Check with your local Census Bureau.) What services are they using? Look in your local Yellow Pages under dating services. Are there any dinner clubs or singles events offered in your area? Check your local newspapers, and utilize the Internet, i.e. Craigslist.org, Singlesonthego.com, etc. What income level will you be dealing with? Based upon the services already offered in your community, what is the average price singles are willing to pay? Do you want to beat that price or up the ante?

Lisa states, "The singles industry is booming—it will never dry up because there will always be single people looking for love."

What service are you offering?

When creating your business plan, consider your niche and price structure as well as a specific outline of the services you will be offering: How many dates/potential matches will you be providing? Will your services be monthly, bi-monthly, yearly? Will you be implementing a coaching program? Will both your male and female clientele pay, or will you cater your services to one gender? Will you be providing events or singles' parties?

Naming the business and setting up office

Before putting your business plan into play you will need a name, phone line, website, and business cards. Perhaps the most important of these is a name. What is the name of your business? It should not only be catchy, memorable, and inviting, but cohesive with your target market. Next, invest in a separate phone line for your services—toll-free is always best. And business cards are a must, as networking is how you will obtain the majority of your clients. Building a website can be a bit pricey, but is now a necessary tool for all businesses.

As a matchmaker you can get away with not having an office. Work from home, and meet your clients at a café or coffee shop. Lisa knows a successful matchmaker who still doesn't have an office. She meets her clients in a café and charges a good deal of money for her services. But if you are meeting in a public space, make sure to arrive early so that you secure a comfortable space to meet your client. Also, make sure to keep your eyes peeled so they don't have to search you out. You want their first meeting with you to be as comfortable as possible.

Getting started

Your matchmaking business begins as soon as you find your first client. You can start as soon as you have one person interested. Take them on as your client, and look for matches specifically for them. As you search, you will automatically be building a database for both your current and future client(s).

However, it is important to understand that when matchmaking professionally, you must reach outside of your personal network of friends—otherwise you won't be making any profit.

Establishing a database

This is where your database comes in. Once you've exhausted every personal connection you have (this includes your friends, friends' friends, family, in-laws, your in-laws' in-laws, your doctors, bankers, hairstylist, etc.)

Lisa's Advice: Think of a potential client, one that you feel will be fairly easy to match. Decide what you'll be charging and then think of friends you may have, neighbors, anyone you know who may be interested. If you can find two potential matches for your client, you've successfully started your business!

it's time to network. Networking is basically another word for socializing—it involves talking to people, exchanging business cards, and getting your name out there.

The best way to do this: parties! Get yourself invited or throw them yourself. Join special interest clubs in your community, become a member on the board of a nonprofit organization, attend grand openings of stores, restaurants, hospitals, and art exhibits. Any type of event with the words reception, mixer, or mingling attached is an opportunity for networking.

As a matchmaker, networking will always be a part of the job description. Event planning is a great business tactic in the beginning, but it may be wise to eliminate it from your business plan once your database grows to a workable size.

As Lisa explains, if you do both matchmaking and events, people will choose to go to your event rather than pay for your services. Matchmaking is more important than throwing events. At events people meet people based on chemistry and looks. But when they hire you, they are making the proactive choice to find someone that is much more appropriate for them for long term compatability. If you can turn a partygoer into a client, then you will be a fabulous matchmaker.

Income

The business of matchmaking can best be compared to the real estate business. Great real estate agents can make a lot of money if they are highly motivated, personable, reliable, and very good at what they do. On the other hand, if a real estate agent is not good, does not work hard, and is not organized, they may make very little money. The business you create is only as good and successful as you are. It takes hard work, motivation, and commitment to grow a new business. As a matchmaker you have to have the ability to sell a contract, to understand the type of market you're working in, and to balance your overhead expenses.

> *Hint:* Some people choose to throw a party themselves. This way they can avoid the 'you don't know me, but I'm a matchmaker' spiel, and automatically become known as the host of a fabulous party. This will increase your exposure as well as your database.

For example, a good real estate agent working in New York City has the potential to make a lot of money, but the overhead may be quite high. Whereas an agent in Iowa also has the potential to make a lot of money—for Iowa. It depends on what you will be charging. What will be your profit margin? What will your overhead cost?

Ask yourself: Do I want an office? Do I want a staff member? How can I make enough money to cover my overhead and make a profit? What extravagances do I want in my life?

Try to keep to a tight budget in the beginning. It is important not to overspend. Put profits back into the business so it can continue to grow.

Lisa states, "Like any new and growing business, you will have to work very hard your first couple of years. But if you're good at what you do—selling, accessing new clients, and networking—you can make a good living."

Getting to Know Your Industry

3

Jerome Chasques loves connecting people to each other. He strongly believes that when you have total strangers share a fun and common experience, they immediately feel related to each other. Jerome successfully organized hundreds of events with creative ways for guests to be introduced to each other (including the acclaimed "Dinner in the Dark" series). But Jerome has also seen firsthand the shortcoming of most singles events and parties—fun is often had, but real connections are seldom made. "I soon realized that you can plan many ways for singles to meet but you can't plan any real chemistry between them without giving them personal attention."

One of the main reasons Lisa and Jerome decided to create the Matchmaking Institute™ was to better define the line between dating services and personalized matchmaking. As a matchmaker you will be entering what is known as the dating or singles market, so it is important for you to have a working knowledge of what it means to be in this industry and the many positions you may choose to take. There are many working business models, all of which may prove valuable to you. By reviewing each existing business model—and evaluating what would work for you—you will achieve a clearer understanding of what your business model should look like, who your competitors may be, and where you will want to position yourself in this environment.

The Revolution of Online Dating

There are over one hundred million singles in the United States today. And in 2003, it was determined that one out of every two singles participated in some form of online dating service. This is great news for matchmakers because it not only means that you're playing to a large audience, but that your audience is responsive. That's over fifty million potential customers! The majority of singles are no longer embarrassed to admit that they're looking for someone. The idea of looking through the personals or accepting a blind date isn't as hush-hush as it might have been ten years ago—or before online dating revolutionized the way we view dating.

From the mass appeal of online dating to the revival of matchmaking

- 1995 – Launch of Match.com
  A revolution in the way people look for love: using a third party
- 1996–1999 – Expansion of online dating
  The multiplication of dating websites removes the stigma of being single and exposed to the world
- 1999 – Launch of the speed dating format
  Looking for someone becomes even more recreational
- 2000–2003 – Online dating peak
  Post 9/11, people's sense of priorities evolve's from professional to personal growth
- 2004–2007 – Revival of "offline" matchmaking
  The new trend of social networking on one side, and a new vision of a modern-day matchmaker as featured on TV or in the press on the other, give a new life to offline dating and personal matchmaking

---

Early dial-up BBS (bulletin board systems) services in the 1980s gave way to America Online in the early 1990s as computers moved to color screens and graphics. Often the driving force behind the BBS services and even America Online was the draw of potential mates. As the Internet became more widely used, other small sites developed. Then in 1995, Match.com created an elaborate site whose sole purpose was to find a date. It was the early days of online personals, and for sure a revolution in the way people were looking for love: Match .com paved the way for the use of a third party to search for a date. It also spawned numerous spin-offs in the singles online market: many other companies began to explore the many ways in which to connect two people. Whether they were looking for romance, adventure, or simply a good time, suddenly singles were no longer intimidated when saying, "I'm single." People were placing their profiles online, making what was once considered private information public, and dating services started holding events specifically for singles.

> *Interesting Fact:* Online dating services received their highest gross number of profiles in the months directly following September 11. "In times of stress and difficulty, people are re-evaluating their priorities, and being in a meaningful relationship is a major priority more so now than in the past" said Rafael Risemberg, a professor of educational psychology at Kean University. "After these tragic events, many people realized that it was important to balance their professional and their personal lives in a different way," adds Jerome.

In 1999, Rabbi Yaacov Deyo launched his speed dating format in Los Angeles in the Orthodox Jewish community. Speed dating gives participants five to seven minutes with each potential match and continues rotating until every single is given the opportunity to meet. The innovation quickly moved across the country from both New York and Los Angeles—and well

19

beyond the Orthodox Jewish community to communities all over the country. Dating services as well as event planning companies received a lot of attention when speed dating became popular. What had started as only a few websites in the early 1990s was by 2004 an industry with literally thousands of services, sites, and event companies all offering to match singles—but what separated one from the other? The popularity of online dating brought about several issues, one of the most severe being privacy. We all have heard stories such as the one about a single woman who set up a date using an online service, but she then discovered that her date was actually her boss. There are also issues with accuracy. People tend to misrepresent themselves especially when it comes to age, height, weight, and occupation. In a sense, the popularity of online dating was also its deficit; with millions of profiles to browse, it became overwhelming as well as questionable.

In 2005, there was a noticeable drop in the growth of the online market. Most sites cut back the number of specific services they offered or eliminated the inclusion of special events, while other companies underwent CEO replacements and overall staff reduction. This made room for personal matchmakers to harness the singles market.

Business Models

It's important for you, as a matchmaker, to be able to differentiate your services from online dating. Here are a few business models to help you understand the singles industry. Note that the singles industry includes online dating services, face-to-face dating services, singles' events, and matchmaking.

On the next page you will find a market segmentation detailing all services representing what we usually call the "dating industry."

Market Segmentation

1. **Online Dating Services**
   online personals / subscription-based or pay-per-contact
   • Match.com, Yahoo! Personals, Friendfinder, Lavalife
     (Member Works, Inc.), AmericanSingles (Spark Networks), Meetic
     (mostly in Europe), etc.
   • Plenty of Fish (an exception since it's free)

2. **Niche Online Dating Services**
   community online personals / pay-per-contact or subscription-based
   • Nerve (Spring Street Networks), Christian Singles, JDate (Spark
     Networks), MillionaireMatch, etc.

3. **Online Relationship Services** (Profile and personality assessment)
   online introduction / subscription-based
   • Introduced by the service:
   • EHarmony, Chemistry, True.com, Perfectmatch
   • Introduced through friends and matchmakers: Engage
   • Introduced by video and website: Great Expectations

4. **Mainstream Offline Introduction Services**
   franchise matchmaking service chains / membership-based
   • Dating Services: It's Just Lunch, Great Expectations
   • Matchmaking Services: MatchMaker International, Together /
     The Right One

5. **Niche Offline Introduction Services**
   niche personal introduction services / membership-based
   • In Good Company, Millionaire's Club, etc.

6. **Face-to-Face Matchmaking**
   personal introduction and relationship services / membership-based
   • 10K+, high-end personal matchmaking (state to be ethical):
     Global Love Mergers, Kelleher & Associates, Selective Search,
     Janis Spindel Serious Matchmaking, Orly the Matchmaker,
     Valenti International, VIP Life, etc.

- 1K to 5K, personal matchmaking (more affordable):
  Leora Hoffman Associates, Shoshanna's Matches, etc.

7. **Matchmaking Event Services**
   dinner parties, + or – intimate format / membership-based
   - Dinner for Six, Dinner at 8, Dinner Dates, etc.

8. **Dating Event Services**
   light and fast format, quantity over quality / Pay-per-event
   - PreDating, Minidates, HurryDate, 8minuteDating, etc.

9. **Singles Events & Activity Groups**
   membership-based or pay-per-event
   - Social Circles, Wine Tastings, Art Lovers, etc.

10. **Social & Business Networking**
    free or pay for premium services
    - Friendster, MySpace, Ryze, Tribe.net, etc.

Online dating services

At the top of their game, leading the online personals are Match.com, Yahoo! Personals, or Lavalife. These services, unlike JDate and Christian Singles, encourage singles from all backgrounds to join. Most online sites follow a similar business plan: They charge an approximate twenty-five-dollar monthly membership fee, and tend to charge more if the member would like to post more pictures or obtain more matches (premier membership). And many of the sites offer special sign-up fees or three or six month bonus packages. One service, Lavalife, has a different business model with a pay-per-credit model.

Online Dating: The Pros and Cons

PROS

Easy to use and convenient
The best Internet dating sites are easy to use. Simple layout: easily upload photos, browse singles' profiles with the option of using an anonymous e-mail address. Online dating services can be accessed whenever you want, twenty-four hours a day.

A potential time-saver
With the majority of people leading busy lives, finding the time to go out and meet new people can be a bit tricky. With a good profile and photo, online dating sites can set you up with plenty of good prospects in your area. This can be achieved in a timely manner.

Builds your social network
Remember that online dating services are not only for finding romance. They're also good for finding like-minded people. Just because the person you've met isn't the "one" for you, they may have friends they can introduce you to and vice versa. Internet dating can be especially helpful when you're new to an area—state, city, or neighborhood.

CONS

Dishonesty
Dishonest people are everywhere, but the Internet provides a good guise. It's a good practice to obtain photographs, exchange e-mails (plural), and talk on the phone before meeting. If you suspect dishonesty, it may be best to move on.

Chemistry
In order to determine whether you have any chemistry with a person, you must physically meet them. Internet dating sites' primary

aim is to help you find compatible singles in your area. They compare wants, preferences, tastes, interests, and personality compatibilities. However, meeting in person is the only way to tell if there's real chemistry.

Inexpensive—but not free
With all good dating services you can sign up for free. However, if you want to initiate contact with others, you must sign up for a membership. These usually range from one month to twelve months.

Online relationship services

Services like Great Expectations (established in 1978) differ from the online personals in that they pre-screen their singles by including either a phone or sit-down interview—this provides the member with minimal human interaction and offers a slightly more personal approach. Once the single is screened, they are then listed online on a secure website for members only. Singles then search for their own matches. Jerome understands this type of humanistic approach to be more of a sales approach: "Basically they have a better chance of convincing you to choose their services if they meet you face-to-face." These services' main objective is to introduce members to other members, with charges sometimes reaching thousands of dollars.

A new kind of relationship services (i.e., relationship as opposed to dating) is taking a new approach, including scientific profile / personality tests developed by authors or experts: eHarmony's Compatibility Matching System, Chemistry's Personality Profile, True's Compatibility Test, or Perfect Match's Duet Total Compatibility System.

Offline introduction services

These dating services can be described as pre-screened introductions with the goal of a second date. With these services, coaching and feedback is very limited. The company couples their members and arranges a lunch or dinner date for them.

The most successful model so far is the one developed by a company named It's Just Lunch. IJL is celebrating nearly sixteen years in the dating business, helping thousands of "busy professional singles." The company was born in 1991 in Chicago and now has locations globally from New York to Singapore, and in between. After founder Andrea McGinty's engagement was called off (and she found herself suddenly single), she began the tedious search to meet "normal," well-educated professionals. Her friends sent her out on blind dates, she tried personal ads, contemplated the Internet and dating services, but she wasn't comfortable with any of these options. The ideal date, she decided, was a lunch date or a drink after work. A fun, laid-back, stress-free way to meet!

> *Tip:* If you haven't decided on a specific niche market yet, these sites will offer plenty of good options. Research these types of services. Take a look at the profiles presented on websites similar to your chosen niche. Are these the type of people you'd like to be working for? Are there a large number of services already catering to your niche? If so, how will you make your services better?

Singles events

Activity clubs, websites, and events offer outings for groups of singles as opposed to one-on-one dates. The company sponsors an event, whether it be scuba diving, hiking, etc., and singles come together while enjoying a common interest. Most companies ask participants to pay per event; however, some offer packaged deals. Activity clubs tend to draw large numbers of singles, but do not have the highest success rate when it comes to actual matches.

These companies couple their members and arrange a lunch or dinner date for three (give or take) paired couples at a time. These companies most often will not pay for the entire meal, but will arrange for a complimentary glass of wine or dessert.

As with all of the business models mentioned, this type of business plan has become popular internationally as well as here in the United States. For example, in Singapore, a matchmaker created a table dating service called Lunchactually.com. Business professionals are matched together on their lunch break, which promotes the idea of a "short and sweet" first date.

Potential matches meet for an hour—just long enough to assess if they'd like to schedule a more formal date, and then they go back to their respective jobs. This business model works well when dealing with an executive clientele—those who are likely to have busier schedules and less time for recreational activities.

Networking services

Another business model, "social networking," arrived on the scene a long time ago but was only popularized in 2002 with the launch of Friendster by entrepreneur Jonathan Abrams. These services are either for professional or social networkers. The websites' basic function is to expand its members' personal circles. Members are invited to put their profiles online and then link to friends, friends of friends, their friends, and so on. Although not specifically geared toward the singles market, many singles enjoy the element of dating within their own circles (even if the person they are dating is more than twenty links away).

Jerome states, "It was revolutionary because it provided a key element that other dating services and websites couldn't offer: trust. With websites like Friendster, a person is guaranteed to be in your circle of friends. It might be someone you don't know at all, but there is a relationship; it's not a perfect stranger."

> *Think of it this way: Would you rather buy a car from someone you know—a friend, family member, or extended relation—or from a total stranger? A friend of yours isn't going to sell you a lemon, but a stranger . . .*

Friendster was one of the first websites to implement this style of profiling, and has had an incredible success rate (31 million profiles as of September 2006). And although the website was built for friends, 90 percent of the site's profilers are single. Networking websites tend to be free to join; they make their money through advertising.

> *Hint:* Social and professional networking sites are an excellent way to build and expand your database.

Personalized matchmaking

The model you'll certainly pay a lot of attention to is "face-to-face matchmaking," and it is the model most likely to fit your needs. What separates you from the rest? You will be rendering a personal service: you will be doing the interviewing; you will be meeting with your clients in your space; you will try to understand exactly what they are looking for; and you will be finding them a match.

Face-to-Face Matchmaking vs. Online Dating

1. Objectivity
- Internet personals are subjective; profiles are not accurate.
- When you meet a matchmaker, your profile is objective and your ID is checked.

2. Time Management
- Browsing hundreds, thousands of online personals . . . and e-mailing back and forth are time consuming.
- Your matchmaker does all the footwork for you. Clients save time and energy.

3. Privacy
- You don't want your boss, your ex-boyfriend, your cousin to know you're looking for someone.

4. Safety
- You don't want to meet a perfect stranger, and you'll feel better meeting someone you've been introduced to, someone whose references have been checked by your matchmaker.

5. Face-to-face
- Nothing can replace meeting someone face-to-face. You just can't know someone online. Any matchmaker will meet face-to-face with their clients and the prospects they match them with; they'll know if these people are shy or not, if they are looking at them in the eyes or not, etc.

Pricing

Pricing is determined by two factors: your client base and how hard you are willing to work. As a matchmaker, you can surpass an income of $100,000—it all depends on how many clients you can manage and your ability to sell. Most matchmakers cater to a client for six- month or yearly periods. Differing from the monthly contract, this allows matchmakers enough time to do a quality search while securing employment for a longer period of time.

You may want to incorporate other services under the umbrella of your matchmaking business. Personal or image coaching will not only bring in more revenue, but will add value to your services. It might also be wise to partner with a complementary business in your industry. For example, partnering with an activity or events company could potentially expand your database and add value to your already valuable services. "Try not to look at other business models as competitors. Learn from them and use them to benefit your business," advises Jerome.

> It is important as a matchmaker to differentiate yourself from the average dating service. Stress to your clients that you personally will be working to find them an appropriate match—not an automated computer program. As a matchmaker you won't be matching likes and dislikes, but personalities to personalities and values to values.

Here's a look at some sample price structures provided by four of the Matchmaking Institute's graduates:

Lunch Actually
Membership in Asia: 1,000
Cost: $780 for six months, six dates minimum; $780–$1,050 for twelve months, twelve dates minimum
Crowd: mid-20s to mid-30s
Selectivity: one-hour introduction interview
Bonus points: members can transfer their membership from one city

to the other.

In2ition
Oceanside, New York
Cost: three introductions for $500; five introductions for $700; eight introductions for $1,000; ten introductions for $1,200 (yearly rates)
Crowd: open to anyone
Bonus Points: Membership includes first date, which takes place at the office. Complimentary coffee and dessert is served.

Sandy Sternbach
New York area: New York, Long Island, Connecticut, New Jersey
Cost: $3,000 retainer for personal search/client services for six months includes four to six introductions and a three-month freeze. $5,000 retainer for personal search/client services includes eight to twelve introductions and a six-month freeze period.
Crowd: baby boomers and seniors; 40+

Dating Directions
Central Ohio membership
Cost: $1,000 to $7,500
Crowd: late 20s and up
Selectivity: two-hour interview and background check
Bonus points: Work with quality singles that are looking for a lifelong relationship.

Crash Course on Signing and Interviewing Clients

4

Making the Most of First Impressions

When speaking with a potential client over the phone, besides setting an appointment, your main objective will be to obtain as much information about him or her as possible:

- How did you hear about this service?
- What do you do for a living?
- What area of town do you live in?
- What is your age?
- Have you ever been married?
- What are you looking for in a mate?

Really listen to their responses, and then ask more questions. And take notes. You can learn a lot about someone in a twenty-minute phone conversation.

By allowing your potential client twenty minutes of your time, you are automatically building a rapport, but more importantly, you will be gathering the information you need to provide the best first impression possible:

- Dress according to their career style—if they are business professionals, they will probably feel more comfortable if you show up in similar attire.
- Choose a meeting place appropriate for both their location and preference (if you do not have an office)—don't suggest a young and trendy café if you're meeting with a lawyer or a doctor.
- Come prepared with a few potential matches based on the preferences they gave you over the phone—this shows that you are already willing to work for them.
- Bring the notes you took while on the phone—during your meeting, reference your phone conversation providing them with a summary of the information you already have. Impress them with your listening skills.

The face-to-face interview

Once you've arranged your meeting (location, time, etc.), the most important thing to remember is . . . be on time! If you've arranged to meet at a café or coffee shop, you should already be seated at a quiet table by the time your client arrives. If you have your own office, prepare any and all paperwork you may need and make it easily accessible. You should also offer water or tea, etc. before starting. The more hospitable, organized, and situated you appear, the more comfortable your client will be.

> *Hint:* People like talking about themselves. All they need is a little provoking . . . and then you can't get them to stop.

Always begin with questions. Ask them how their day is going so far. Ask them what they are currently working on at their job. And act interested.

Your first questions should most definitely be about their chosen profession. This gives them the opportunity to warm-up in a way—it's personal, but not too personal. Allow them to do most of the talking, interjecting every once in a while to make sure they know you're hearing them.

> Do not talk about yourself, and do not try to relate their relationship stories to yours. A common question from potential clients is, "Are you married?" A simple yes or no will suffice. Remember—this is about them, not you.

Once you've moved on from work and onto their relationship history, the same rules apply. Ask questions, listen to the responses; ask more questions, repeat or summarize for them what they've told you. For example:

"So what you're telling me is . . ."

"I understand you're feeling . . . and you would like to find . . ."

Make no judgments and allow them to tell you what they want in a mate—even if you think you already know.

The myth of the one-day close

Don't be fooled! Seventy percent of potential clients who walk away from the initial meeting without signing a contract . . . will change their minds! Allow them their space, and don't oversell. If you've done your job correctly, they will most likely give you a call within the next twenty-four hours. Encourage potential clients to go home and think about it—you'll give them a follow-up call in a couple of days.

If the answer is still "no," walk away. After all, you don't want to work for someone who has reservations from the get-go.

Selling your client

In the business of selling, it is important to believe in your product—the same goes for matchmaking. And the ability to match your client is comparable to your ability to sell a product. To successfully sell a product, a salesman will always point out the product's best qualities. It is your job to find the best qualities in your client. At times, these qualities will be obvious—good-looking, successful, interesting, social, etc. And then there will be times when you have to dig a little deeper to find the selling qualities. For example, is he extremely passionate about the environment? Does he love to cook? Is he extremely intelligent? These are examples of the qualities that compose a person's personality, and it is these qualities that will help you find an appropriate match.

Keep in mind, however, that you are in fact selling a person, not a product; emotions will be involved, and vulnerability levels high.

It is important as a matchmaker to connect on a personal level with each of your clients. This can be very difficult, which is why remaining objective is key. Perhaps you don't connect with your client's passion for politics; you should still recognize this quality as a selling point, and many other people will find this quality attractive. Remaining business-like and professional is important, and it will often prove advantageous to view your clients in these terms.

Remaining optimistic and available

Many of your clients may be coming from a place of hurt. Perhaps they have just gone through a break-up, or maybe they're tired of feeling alone. As a matchmaker, it is your job to point out the positive. Remind them that they've made a proactive choice, and things can only get better.

If your client has gone on a few dates, and still hasn't found his or her match, he or she will most likely become less than resolute. This is when your personal coaching skills will be put to the test. Remain optimistic and upbeat, never allowing a hint of negativity to creep in.

A large part of matchmaking centers on dialogue—dialogue between you and your client—which is why you must make yourself available. Clients will want your advice on everything from which person to date to which outfit to wear. They will need to provide you with feedback for each of their dates before you can set them up with another. Your clients' schedules will change as well as their dating preferences—trust me, this will all happen, and you'll have to be there.

Provide your clients with a number where they can always reach you, and always call two to three days after they've had a date. E-mail works too, and it's a great way to receive feedback from your client. Paper trails are always helpful.

Quality Control: The Interview Process

Eight years ago, Jill Weaver responded to a listing for Matchmaking International, which was then a larger-scale matchmaking service utilizing the talent of both matchers and interviewers (or what they referred to as "sales associates"). With six matchers and four sales associates, Matchmaking International served a higher volume of clients and functioned on a less personal level than most smaller matchmaking services. Jill worked as a matcher for the company and immediately fell in love with her newly chosen profession. Her background in sociology and psychology aided her already natural ability to match singles—her passion for matchmaking having taken root as an adolescent.

In November 2003, Jill bought a franchise of Matchmaking International, restructuring their high-volume business model to bring her branch down to a more personal level. She traded in her office suite for the opportunity to work from home, and rather than relying on matchers and sales associates, she currently acts as the primary matchmaker, with the help of one administrative assistant.

Jill jokingly refers to herself as a "soccer mom" when asked about her two children. Because of her home-office setup, Jill incorporates both "mommy" and matchmaking skills into her daily routine. Oftentimes clients will come in for an interview to be greeted by Jill, her assistant, and her eighth grader's science project. Because work and home are so closely related, Jill feels the most important part of her job is prescreening and interviewing—both of which help to insure quality clientele.

Prescreening your clients

Before inviting a potential client to meet with you, there are a number of things you can learn about them by simply conversing over the phone. During the phone conversation, ask yourself: Does this client fit my business's criteria? Does this client have the potential to benefit from my services? Does this person sound like someone I will enjoy working with? Can this person afford my fees? With these key questions in mind, you will conduct an interview over the phone.

The first question for your potential client should always be: How did you hear about my services? As a business owner, it is always nice to know where your potential clients are coming from, whether a friend referred them to you or they saw your flier at an event they recently attended—this type of information can and should be used to track marketing.

Follow this question with: And what kind of information can I give you? Jill explains that at this point in the conversation it is your time to out-talk them—your main objective being to schedule a time and place for your face-to-face interview. I encourage you to meet with potential clients free of charge. It's not that your time isn't worth anything, but most people will be pleasantly surprised to find they can meet with you for free. Invite your clients to simply come in and talk so that together you can figure out if matchmaking is something that will work for you.

Many people truly believe they want a relationship. But the truth is, they just aren't ready. Many of us try to fill the voids in our life with a relationship, when in reality we must first deal with the other issues at hand. Do your best to decipher whether the person on the phone is truly open and ready for your help.

Basic Information to Gather During a Prescreening Phone Call:

- First name
- Age
- Marital status
- Occupation
- Contact information
- Children
- Requirements in a match

Reiterate to your clients that all information given to you is 100 percent confidential.

Setting a date

You can talk on the phone with a potential client for hours, but try to keep it as short and simple as possible—make it long enough to develop a rapport, but cut it short once the majority of the conversation becomes dominated by them. Assure them that you will further detail everything they would like to know during the face-to-face interview. Ask them, "What's better for you? Evenings, days, weekends?" Before you know it, they're booked.

Before ending your phone call, make sure you get a phone number where they can be reached and call the evening before your face-to-face interview to confirm time and location. As Jill explains, "This is helpful for two reasons. One—it is a way to get in contact with them in the off chance they are running late or fail to show. Two—it's the second step in developing a rapport with that person."

Interviewing Outline:

1. Rapport Building:
Your handshake should be firm but not too aggressive. Remember to always smile and start with small talk:
"Were my directions okay?"
"How are you currently meeting people?"
"How did you hear about us?"
"What brings you here today?"

2. Introductory:
Restate your business description:
"We are a professional, personalized introduction service." Explain your agenda. "Today I am going to start by getting some basic information from you, then I will show you exactly how and why our program works, and we can find the package that suits you best." Then you can say something like: "There will be some worksheets to fill out. They're actually kind of fun."

3. Your Questionnaire:
Your questionnaire can be several pages and should include questions about age, employment, children, religion, etc., as well as hobbies and interests.

4. Personal Values Rating List:
Based on the Jung-Myers-Briggs typology. Ask your clients to rate the personal qualities and characteristics they'd prefer their match to embody, according to levels of importance.

5. Background Check:
Background checks are a safety precaution you may or may not choose to use—just make sure your client signs a release form. You will need to obtain both their license/ID number and Social Security number.

The interviewing process

When it comes to interviewing, you will of course have your very own personal style. The questions you ask and how well you get to know your potential client is entirely up to you. When allotting time for interviews, Jill suggests you give your interviewee as much of your time as you can possibly spare. After all, we are all very complex human beings, and the amount of information that you may be able to use as a matchmaker is endless.

Sample pre-screening form for you to complete during the interview:

Matchmaking Institute
The School of Matchmaking & Relationship Sciences

Screen and Qualify

Interviewer_____ Referral Source _____ Date _____

Name (First) _____ (Last) _____

Address _____ City _____ St_____ Zip _____

Home Phone _____ Work _____ Cell _____

Email _____ preferred phone _____okay to leave msgs_____

DOB _____ Age _____ Status S W D Sep How Long _____ County _____

Height _____Weight _____ Hair _____ Eye Color _____Religion _____ OCG RCG

Number of Children _____ Ages _____ Custody Arrangement _____

Education HS ____ College _____ Degrees _____ Major _____ Other _____

Occupation _____ How Long _____ Salary _____

Health _____ Current Medications or Restrictions _____ Smoke: ___ Prefer to Date _____

Drink ____ Light___ Social___ Regular_____ Last Serious Relationship _____

How have you been meeting people in the past? _____

If we were to match you with someone ideal, would you be available to meet that person in 2-3 weeks? _____

Qualities you are looking for in a mate: Age range _____ Height Range _____

Weight Range _____ Type: Athletic _____ Non-athletic _____ Physical Build _____

Children _____ Marital Status: S W Div Sep Religion _____ Educ Level: HS College Degree

Interested in Marriage _____ Interested in Children _____ Interested in future children _____

Area (Networking) _____ Distance you willing to travel _____

Drivers License # _____ Social Security # _____

Comments _____

_____

Screen-Qualify.doc

Matchmaking Institute™ Inc.
The School of Matchmaking & Relationship Sciences™
www.MatchmakingInstitute.com

89 Fifth Avenue, Suite 602
New York, NY 10003
Info@MatchInstitute.com
Tel: 212-242-0965

Sample interest/hobbies list for your client to complete during the interview:

Leisure Interests/Hobbies

Below is a list of interests and hobbies. Please rate them according to your interest level.

Item	No Interest	Some Interest	Would Go/Do	Like It	Love It!
Alpine Skiing					
Archeology					
Architecture					
Art					
Auto Racing					
Biking					
Bowling					
Camping					
Classical Music					
Comedy					
Conversation					
Country Music					
Cross Country Skiing					
Dancing					
Dining Out					
Fine Wines					
Fishing					
Flying (Private Plane)					
Golf					
Hiking					
Jazz Music					
Jet Skiing					
Jogging					
Live Theater					
Motorcycles					
Movies					
Museums					
Musicals					
Musicals					
Opera					
Parasailing					
Photography					
Playing Cards					
Politics					
Popular Music					
Racquetball					
Rap/Hip Hop					
Reading					
Rock Music					
Sailing					
Singing					
Swimming					
Television					
Tennis					
Travel – Domestic					
Travel - International					
Water Skiing					
Weight training					

Name: _____   Date: _____

LeisureInterests.doc

41

Key questions you should always ask

What are you looking for in a potential mate? This is a loaded question. Not only will you be able to conclude if your database has the potential to offer appropriate matches, but their preferences will tell you a great deal about what type of person they are. If they supply you with a laundry list of requirements, it is generally safe to assume they are prone to self-insecurities. If your potential client has an extremely difficult time answering this question, he or she is most likely a very passive and indecisive person. Both personality types have the potential to be difficult clients to please.

> A lot of people are looking to be heard, to feel good about themselves, for somebody to truly bring out their essence. So, even though that man claims he wants the pretty woman—the trophy—by reaching a little bit farther, you will be able to see that what he really wants is to feel good about himself.

Do you smoke? If not, do you find smoking to be a turn-off? Smoking is a big issue for many people. If the client smokes, ask if he or she is a light, respectful smoker or an addict. If he or she doesn't, ask how important it is that a potential match be a nonsmoker. For the majority of nonsmokers, smoking will be what many matchmakers call a "deal-breaker." "Deal-breakers," Jill explains, "are those issues that the client is not willing to budge on. For example, a potential match may meet all of my client's requirements—all but the deal-breaker. Therefore, I will not introduce them."

If I were to find a potential match for you within the next two weeks, would you be available? By asking this question, you let your potential client know that you are ready and willing to start working for them. This question also sets the ball in motion, so to speak; it plants the seed. By now, your client should be thinking about meeting people—the excitement of future possibilities sinking in.

Closing the deal

Hiring a matchmaker is an investment—an investment of time, money, energy, and heart. Let your potential client know how thankful you are that you were given the opportunity to meet with them, and congratulate them for taking the leap with you. Remind them that nothing has been carved in stone; changes and adjustments to their profile, preferences, schedule, etc. can always be made. Assure them you will be contacting them in the next few days . . . and you're on your way.

They're happy. You're happy. Let the matching begin.

Some people, no matter what, are going to say they have to think about it. That's okay. You're asking them to take a leap of faith. As with all matters of the heart—sometimes we need a little more time.

Interviewing Skills
Highlights—be mindful of the following!

- It's your interview and you are the director. Stay on course. Redirect if you need to. It is not advantageous to listen to a client's last two years of heartaches, but do establish the need and benefit of your service. With compassion, gently reinforce, "That's why it's so great that you are here today."

- Be honest. Never jeopardize your integrity by overselling. Do not claim marriage in one year. If you are interviewing a client that will be difficult to match, express that. Difficult is not impossible. It just requires additional patience and understanding. Example—overweight clients, or smokers.

- Know that you don't need to know everything! You only need to know your program inside and out . . . you are not a fortune teller. Each person will have their own experience, because individual criteria are specific. Remind client, it only takes one right match for a successful relationship

- It's okay to share some of you. It may be the ingredient that is needed to create a comfortable atmosphere. Keep it small and generic. Example of inappropriate sharing: "Yeah, I remember when my ex cleared out our bank account . . ." Not okay, too much information.

- It's okay to brag about your service, tastefully! Display wedding announcements, thank you notes, and published articles. It will make your business more credible. Do not discredit another service.

- Never breach confidentiality. It can be tempting! If you need to debrief, do so externally (outside of your work environment).

- Most importantly, have fun with your interview!! (ABCs: Attitude, Body language, Content.) Your attitude sets the tone. Be upbeat, open, and informative.

- Reassurance and appreciation does wonders! "Thank you so much for coming in today. I'm so glad we met . . ."

The Method Behind the Matches

5

Most people use their instincts or intuition when choosing a life partner. As a matchmaker, you will undoubtedly rely on the same feeling or "hunch" when pairing couples together. The ability to intrinsically produce matches will prove to be an incredible advantage to you. However, the skill of coupling can also be taught by using structure and logic.

Steven Sacks, the author of *The Mate Map: The Right Tool for Choosing the Right Mate*, believes that although many happy unions are created instinctually, there is a particular structure that one may use when deciding which pair will make a good match.

The State of Mate Selection

When it comes to finding true love, most people expect things to happen naturally; for a spark to one day ignite, and from then on to live happily ever after. Perhaps it's not really our fault that we feel this way—we see it in the movies all the time, so why shouldn't it happen for us in real life? But from a logical perspective, this way of thinking does not make sense. Steven explains that "most often people don't know what they want in a mate until they've stumbled upon the right one, or are recently reeling from the wrong one. So, the idea is to get people to think about the details of relationships before they end up in one that may not be right for them."

To decide whether or not a person is "right" can seem daunting, but when broken down into smaller decisions, the question becomes much more answerable.

As a person goes through the dating process, it is really a series of smaller questions: Do I want to go on a first date with this person? A second? A third? The answer to each smaller question will indicate and eventually lead to the answer for the overall question: Is this person a potential long-term mate for me?

So, how do you get your clients to think about these things?

"Seventy-five percent of us are visual learners. When you put things on paper, it just sinks in that much more. So, I would urge you to have your clients do the same," Steven says.

As you ask your clients for feedback after they've been on a date have them write a list of what they liked and disliked. By encouraging them to document their feelings, you are helping them to take a more structured approach to love.

Looking at the bigger picture

It will also help if you urge your clients to look beyond common interests. People tend to rate levels of compatibility based on the number of activities or hobbies they can both enjoy together. Steven explains this is really just a default mechanism people use when asked to describe what they are looking for in a mate. Common interests have the ability to bring two people together, but do not carry enough weight to make a relationship successful. For example, a relationship may start with a shared passion for the theater, and then grow from there. But a relationship should not start with a common interest, and continue as the result of further common interests. Common interests make getting to know someone fun, but is not a predictor of long-term compatability. Steven explains that "people should have one or two common hobbies they can enjoy together—but this is just part of the picture, not the main element."

Improving the system

Besides relying on a matchmaker, there are numerous services people can use, each of which relies on its own matching system. The majority of systems use likes, dislikes, and shared interests to form what looks like a laundry list. Steven has created a structured system in which clients can not only list their preferences, but also rate the importance of each physical characteristic and personality trait. This urges clients to be more upfront with both you and themselves, allowing for a quicker and more appropriate matching.

Profile attributes

These attributes are the basic factual information that you need to know about your client and the person they would like to meet. There are eight profile attributes. These are age, career/job, educational level, ethnicity, geographic desirability, religion, socioeconomic status, and hobbies/interests. These will help narrow down some basic requirements for finding a match for your client. Ask your client to provide the level of importance in each of these areas. For example, how important is geographical location? Is your client willing to date someone out of their area? If so, how far?

Relationship essentials

"I believe that in order for two people to last in a relationship, they need to be compatible in four key areas. They are personality, physical attraction, love, and chemistry. If two people don't

have a high level of each of these things, the relationship will not last," asserts Steven.

Physical and personality attributes

When it comes to physical attraction, everyone has a sense of their general "type." The more specific you can get your clients to be about physical characteristics in the beginning, the better off you'll both be. There are sixteen physical attributes to help you clients prioritize. They are hair, eyes, face, smile, lips, teeth, nose, ears, skin, height, body, sex appeal, cuteness, prettiness/handsomeness, femininity/masculinity, and overall look. This is considered the outer beauty of the person. So for example, are good teeth extremely important to a client? Are full lips crucial? If a client tells you the level of importance of these key physical elements it will serve as a very useful tool as to what your client will find attractive and where they are flexible.

Personal Preference: When people describe what they are looking for in a relationship-personality-wise, physical attribute-wise—you can't tell anyone what they want is wrong. It really comes down to personal preference. When matchmaking, it is important to encourage personal preference. You don't want to drive anyone away by interjecting too many of your opinions.

The same goes for personality. Personality, however, is extremely in-depth and far more difficult to match. The personality fit each of us wants is different from that of every other person, because there are so many attributes and so many individual desires and needs. It's often the case that an attribute that appeals to one person turns another person off. Although several attributes such as being kind-hearted and trustworthy are typically considered desirable, overall personality fit is based mostly on personal choice. You have to get to know your client individually to understand what his or her personality preference is.

On the following two pages you will find sample worksheets, useful tools that will help you to learn more about your clients preferences. This information will be very valuable when narrowing down your search and deciding on appropriate matches for your clients.

© The Mate Map (www.matemap.com)

Matchmaking Institute
The School of Matchmaking & Relationship Sciences

The Science of Matching

To help us match you with someone you will find desirable, please complete the following in order of preference.

For the attributes, choose your first, second and third level of preference. We will try to match you with your first preference, but if we are unable to find an adequate overall match, we will match your with your second preference, and then, if need be, match you with your third preference. As you go from your first preference to your second and third preferences, you may find that you become more flexible.

Section A — *Profile Attributes*

Examples	First Preference	Second Preference	Third Preference
Age	27-31	25-32	25-34
Religion	Catholic	Catholic	Catholic/Protestant
Ethnicity	Caucasian	Any	Any
Education	Graduate Degree	Bachelors Degree	Associate Degree
Previous Marriage	Never Been Married	Any	Any
Any Children	No Kids	No Kids	No Kids
Location (miles from you)	10 miles	Same City	Same State

	First Preference	Second Preference	Third Preference
Age			
Religion			
Ethnicity			
Education			
Previous Marriage			
Any Children			
Location (miles from you)			

Section B — *Physical Attributes*

Examples	First Preference	Second Preference	Third Preference
Height	5'4" – 5'6"	5'3" – 5'8"	5'3" – 5'10"
Body Type	Slender	Slender, Average	Slender, Average
Eyes	Blue	Blue	Any
Hair Color	Blonde	Blonde/Black	Any
Hair Style	Long, Medium	Long, Medium	Long, Medium, Short
Teeth/Smile	Excellent, Very Good	Excellent, Very Good, Good	Excellent, Very Good, Good
Skin	Excellent, Very Good	Excellent, Very Good, Good	Excellent, Very Good, Good
Lips	Normal	Normal, Full	Any

	First Preference	Second Preference	Third Preference
Height			
Body Type			
Eyes			
Hair Color			
Hair Style			
Teeth/Smile			
Skin			
Lips			

So, in this example here, your first preference is looking for somone who's age 27–31. Your second preference is 25–32 and third preference is 25–34. So, really, your third preference is your bottom line, what you are not willing to bend on, or the deal-breaker.

Matchmaking Institute
The School of Matchmaking & Relationship Sciences

Section C   Personality Attributes

Step 1

Below are 29 pairs of personality attributes, where one extreme is called the left pole attribute and the other extreme is called the right pole attribute. For each of the 29 pairs, mark the box on the 6-point scale that describes _you_ best. For example, your choices for Optimistic—Pessimistic are Most Optimistic, Very Optimistic, Somewhat Optimistic, Somewhat Pessimistic, Very Pessimistic, Most Pessimistic.

Example:

Left Pole Attribute	Most	Very	Somewhat	Somewhat	Very	Most	Right Pole Attribute
Affectionate		X					Not Affectionate
Assertive					X		Not Assertive
Calm				X			Hotheaded
Decisive		X					Indecisive

Please Complete:

Left Pole Attribute	Most	Very	Somewhat	Somewhat	Very	Most	Right Pole Attribute
Affectionate							Not Affectionate
Assertive							Not Assertive
Calm							Hotheaded
Decisive							Indecisive
Disciplined							No self control
Energetic							Mellow
Follows Rules							Rebellious
Handles Adversity Well							Handle Adversty Poorly
Career Ambition							No career ambition
High Maint.							Low Maint.
High Sex Drive							Low Sex Drive
Honesty							Dishonest
Independent							Dependent
Industrious							Lazy
Intelligent							Not Intelligent
Kind Hearted							Uncaring
Makes Me Laugh							Does Not Make Me Laugh
Neat							Messy
Optimistic							Pessimistic
Private							Revealing
Proactive							Procrastinating
Religious							Not Religious
Responsible							Irresponsible
Saver							Spender
Sensative							Thick Skinned
Sociable							Not Sociable
Spiritual							Not Spiritual
Talkative							Quiet
Worldly							Naive

Step 2   For all 29 pairs, decide which 10 are Extremely Important to you and highlight them.

Left Pole Attribute	Most	Very	Somewhat	Somewhat	Very	Most	Right Pole Attribute
Affectionate		X					Not Affectionate
Assertive					X		Not Assertive
Calm				X			Hotheaded

Step 3   Now select the attributes you want in a partner by marking the boxes with a circle.

Left Pole Attribute	Most	Very	Somewhat	Somewhat	Very	Most	Right Pole Attribute
Affectionate		X					Not Affectionate
Assertive					X		Not Assertive
Calm				X			Hotheaded

© *The Mate Map (www.matemap.com)*

Once your client has completed both worksheets, you will be able to match according to their first, second, and third preferences. When you go through the system, you are going to try to match people based on their first preference, but if you can't, at least you have the ability to widen the pool of candidates for them.

Chemistry and love

Chemistry and love are different than personal and physical attraction; these are two key elements you really can't plan for. But there are ways to help your clients recognize the signs and feelings these elements emit. As a matchmaker, you will be dealing mostly with chemistry. Love is much harder to predict.

So let us look at chemistry. Although it is often thought that two people either have chemistry or they don't, it isn't really so black and white. This is because chemistry is not just one overall entity, but instead is made up of six different categories. We can have a high level of chemistry in one category with someone and a low level in another category with that same person. The six chemistry categories are verbal communication, nonverbal communication, sexual compatibility, desire to be together, ease of getting along, and influence. You can help your clients review each area of chemistry they felt with each of the matches you have introduced to them. This will help you begin to understand what areas are more important to your client as well as what areas they are strong in.

Natural Chemistry

Chemistry Categories	Examples of Excellent or Very Good Chemistry
Verbal Communication The Clarity of your verbal interactions	When I explained what the favor I asked of him entailed, he understood me completely and took care of everything the way I wanted it to be.
	We are so in synch that I no longer need to finish my sentences because she understands what I am saying.
	Our conversations flow with ease.
Non-Verbal Communication How you connect through eye contact, touch and body language	The instant I shot her a look room across the table, she knew that she should change the subject.
	If I'm feeling down, he can make me feel better by a simple touch.
	When we are at a party and on opposite sides of the room, I can feel his eyes on me while I'm talking to friends and my back is turned to him.
Sexual Compatibility How well you fit sexually	I don't ever want to stop kissing him because it makes me feel so great.
	I felt completely comfortable the first time we were naked together.
	Even when I'm busy and not "in the mood", she still turns me on and I want to take her clothes off.

© *The Mate Map (www.matemap.com)*

53

Chemistry Categories	Examples of Excellent or Very Good Chemistry
Makes Me Better How well he or she naturally improves you	He makes me feel as if I can accomplish anything. I've never had such a positive outlook on life before. I am always so comfortable around her, whether we are alone or with other people. I find myself more expressive and open when I am with him.
Ease of Getting Along How comfortable you are with him or her	I feel that we've known each other for years, although we've only been dating a short time. When we are together, I'm comfortable with long periods of silence. She rarely gets on my nerves.
Intensity To Be Together Your need to spend time with him or her	When he went out of town for three days, I longed for him more than I expected. Even the thought of seeing her later today puts a smile on my face. We always have such a great time together, that it's not the same when I have plans without him.

© *The Mate Map (www.matemap.com)*

54

Love Categories	Examples of Excellent or Very Good Love
Importance How important of a role does he or she play in your life	I factor in what he would want in most decisions I make, even when a decision only affects him marginally.
	When talking to my girlfriends, I refer to him (almost bragging about him) several times throughout the conversation.
	I am willing to compromise on issues that I wouldn't have compromised on previously, because I want him to get his way also.
Changes Me for the Better How he or she changes your outlook	Thanks to her, a significant other has now become a more important aspect of my life.
	He makes me believe I can accomplish anything I want to.
	Knowing that someone so wonderful loves me makes me look at myself in a positive way.
Love Compatibility How well he or she fits with you	I have a great amount of respect for her, which I have not felt with other girlfriends.
	I believe in him.
	She values the things about me that I value most in myself.

© *The Mate Map (www.matemap.com)*

With the profile, spectrum, and physical attribute, you can help your client understand what they want in a mate even before dating someone. This will help you narrow down matches and make better decisions for your client, making the possibility for successful matches greater.

If all goes well and your clients finds love, it is wise to discuss with them the signs of love before they put their membership on hold. Love is defined as having deep feelings of affection and emotional intensity toward a potential or current mate. Although it is often thought that two people are either in love or they're not, love isn't really so black and white. This is because love is not just one overall entity, but instead is made up of six deferent categories. We can have a high level in one category and a low level of love in another category with that same person. The six love categories are: what you feel, importance, what you find special (or not special), love fulfillment, love compatibility, and changes in outlook for the better (or worse).

Finding the perfect match for you client is not 100 percent science, instinct, or analysis, but the more tools you have to make these choices, the more accurate you can be when helping your client find love.

Making a Name for Yourself

6

Networking

Developing your networking skills is essential to becoming a successful matchmaker. You will not only need these skills to secure clientele, but to build a sufficient database as well. The good news—we network everyday! It may help you to think of networking as socializing. Anytime you've ever met someone new, exchanged phone numbers or e-mail addresses, you've networked.

Networking provides a plethora of advantages to a small business owner such as yourself. For starters, expanding your network can be compared to expanding your advertising budget. The word of mouth approach is an extremely valuable marketing tool, and the more people you know, the more people they know, and the more people who know about your services. Talk to people; talk to people wherever you go; go where you'll be able to talk to people! The more connections you make, the larger your database and clientele will grow.

It's always nice to have friends in high places. Your ultimate goal in networking will be to seek out the people who will be able to help you. Whether you're looking for a potential match or someone to financially back your next event, your objective will be to find those with something valuable to offer.

Growing your network

Your family and friends are already part of your network. Perhaps your network is already quite large; perhaps it's on the smaller side. No matter what the scope, there is always room for expansion. Start with your immediate circle and work to stem outward. Reconnect with old colleagues and classmates. Call or write your distant relatives. Make friends with your in-laws. E-mail everyone on your contact list.

Become a social butterfly

Keeping your potential clientele in mind, peruse the local papers for any and all events where you'll be able to network. Join both business and leisure activity groups; find a cause, attend charity and fundraising events.

You should be out networking at least twice a week!!

Stand out in a crowd

So, you've honed in on your potential clientele, meaning you've discovered the perfect event to attend; one that will supply the perfect opportunity to network—now what?

Show up early—this not only allows you to stake out the crowd as they arrive, but also provides the perfect opportunity to mingle with the event organizers. If they're taking care of last-minute details when you arrive, offer your help. Party planners and event organizers are important people to know.

Talk to strangers—introduce yourself to as many people as you can and ask questions. People love to talk about themselves. Ask them what they're drinking. Inquire as to why they decided to attend this particular event, and how they're affiliated. Allow the conversation to flow naturally, and when they ask for your profession, then and only then should you explain.

Never begin a conversation with: "Hi, I'm a matchmaker."

Exchange business cards—always be prepared to pull out your card at a moment's notice. Invest in a business card holder with two compartments: one for inputting, one for outputting. And never leave home without it! Throughout the event try to exchange business cards with everyone you speak to.

Debriefing—as soon as you get home or back to the office, it is imperative that you go through the business cards you collected from that event. While the evening's conversations are still fresh in your mind, write something memorable about that person on the back of their card. For example, "Donna Smith" talked about her twelve-year-old son non-stop. Write it down along with what possible help she can provide to you.

Maintaining your network

A phone number and an e-mail address hold no value if you don't use them. Always think of reasons to contact your contacts: birthdays, condolences, congratulations, invitations, etc. For example, if you have recently made a financial contact, ask for his or her advice when you update your business plan—anything to keep the lines of communication open and the possibility for growth alive.

Suggested Industry and Social Networking Groups

- **Social networking:** Ryze.com, LinkedIn.com, Tribe.net, Ecademy.com
- **Alumni:** Classmates.com
- **Friends:** Friendster.com, MySpace.com
- **Business Circles:** finance, HR, senior execs, marketing
- **Other sample groups:** AlwaysOn.goingon.com, Meetup.com, TheSquare.com, eWomenNetwork.com, MBAAssociation.org, Groups.Yahoo.com, Topica.com, Craigslist.org

Public Relations

Celebrities wouldn't be half as famous if it weren't for their publicists. A publicist is in charge of marketing a person's image. The majority of articles you read and the pictures you see of so-called superstars can most often be linked to a good publicist or PR firm. As a matchmaker, you will need to serve as your own publicist. This means selling yourself to the media in exchange for exposure and credibility.

Hint: Hire a photographer to take a professional photograph of you. This type of photo is known as a headshot. Note we did not say glamour shot. And we most certainly did not say mug shot! Your headshot may be used for your website and advertisements, and should always be included in your press kit.

Upholding a sense of professionalism

People may not always take you as seriously as you'd like . . . or as you'd expect. As you may have gathered, matchmaking is not the most typical of professions, but this does not mean you shouldn't be shown the same amount of respect a lawyer or doctor would receive.

To describe one's self as a "professional" is

not so much a definition, but more a representation of standards. As it relates to business, the word personifies an idea of formality and standard procedure: Society expects a "professional" to dress, behave, and communicate in a particular manner. We are not suggesting that you should in any way compromise your identity, but it will prove beneficial to your business if you maintain industry standards.

Because the majority of your communication will be phone and Internet based, it is important to practice proper written and verbal etiquette.

Tips for looking professional when communicating by e-mail

- Get a permanent e-mail address and domain name.
- Do not use an Internet service provider's e-mail address.
- Maintain two e-mail accounts (personal/business).
- Use a signature file.
- Observe e-mail etiquette.
- Master your subject line.

Meeting the media

In order to become marketable to the media industry, you must first become familiar with any and all sources of press related to your particular field. Magazines, newspapers, and radio shows may be viewed as potential marketing tools so it is your job to find the publications in which it might behoove both you and the publisher to feature a story about matchmaking.

Once you've found your potential media "ins," request their editorial calendars and research their writers, contributing staff, and columnists. Research possible events in your area where local journalists are apt to attend, and practice your networking skills.

Building your press kit

When it comes to contacting the media, your press kit serves as your calling card. The press kit acts as your written introduction, representing what you do, why, and how you do it. The materials in your press kit should be presented in a professional way providing the receiver with concisely written, grammatically clean copy.

Your press kit should come equipped with a simple biography, which includes your reason for becoming a matchmaker.

Getting Ready to Speak Out
Write these things out for yourself

- Your personal history (background, why you became a matchmaker . . .)
- Your personal & business values
- Your business orientations (choosing your targets)
- Your business added-value (how to differentiate yourself from competitors)

Ask a few of your clients if they would be willing to write a testimonial for you, praising your ability as a matchmaker. By including these in your press kit, you will be providing the publication with a form of credibility.

When it comes to writing feature articles, journalists are always looking for the human element. Do you have any interesting stories about your work as a matchmaker? They will also want to see the ways in which your services differ from your competitors. Journalists are tough sells. You have to give them a reason to write about you. What makes you special? Why will their readers want to read about you?

Basic Rules When Speaking to Journalists

- It's not about you or your business, but about the solutions you bring.
- It's not about your schedule, but about the right media timing: Valentine's Day, Mother's or Father's Day (single parents), etc.
- No matter what, be positive and enthusiastic.
- Use criticism to your advantage; accept it as a challenge and prove them wrong.
- Don't behave or speak like a sales person—journalists hate this!

Of course, your number one priority as a matchmaker will be to match clients, but just because you're about to become one of the busiest and most successful matchmakers out there doesn't mean you can't and shouldn't make time for a little PR. Acting as your own publicist won't always be easy. Don't get discouraged. Remember there are people out there whose whole career revolves around public relations—and we're asking you to do both matchmaking and PR! However, with a little bit of time and effort, you will have the ability to skyrocket your business.

Solutions for Time Constraints and Other Issues

- Allow yourself some time each week to network and master your PR skills.
- Read magazines (professional, business, local).
- Identify media relevant (local television, radio, press) to your business.
- Write down names of staff writers or freelancers (and Google them).
- Call to receive editorial calendars.
- Develop your contacts.
- Grow your network, mingle.
- Become a guest speaker.
- Write a newsletter.
- Go to events that journalists might attend.

PART II

Matchmakers' Stories

Matchmaking Experience: A First-Hand Account

by Rob Anderson

7

Starting from Square One

When I entered the field of matchmaking I entered from the other side—not as a matchmaker, but as a match. The then director of Club Elite, the company I now work for, approached me at an event and asked me, "Are you single? Because I would love to set you up with one of my clients." I was flattered and agreed to go on the date with his client. The date didn't work out, but the career opportunity of a lifetime did. I was offered a position and have now been a matchmaker for almost four years.

When I first started, I was trained by the owner of the company and later took the matchmaker certification course provided by the Matchmaking Institute™. Once I became an officially certified matchmaker, I was left to my own devices. I was at a great vantage point—I was taking over an established company rather than starting my own. But like all new matchmakers, I faced the challenge of making a name for myself. Although technically an established matchmaking service, we had neither the clientele nor the recognition we needed. Nobody knew who we were.

Spinning the web

"I found that networking was really the most important part of the whole job."

So the question was: "How do I take this company and turn it into something?"

I needed to find clients and I needed to find matches. So I started with the people I already knew—the people in my immediate network. Then I began attending events on a weekly basis. Since the company focuses on a specific niche market, it has certain advantages over a more general service. Being that my niche market is the gay male, there is more of a community with resources for gay men and it makes it easier to choose events that target my market. I chose to attend a gay and lesbian meeting for "out" professionals. The meeting was centered on a guest lecturer, with a cocktail hour held prior, which is key for networking.

As I walked into the event, my heart was pounding and my palms were sweating. I assumed the worst: I figured they would think I was crazy. I thought, "What am I going to do? Walk up to strangers and say, 'Hi, I'm a matchmaker, I run a company, and I don't know how to do this but do you want to date one of my clients?'" But I was pleasantly surprised. The guests proved to be very receptive, and most were genuinely flattered when I approached them. I quickly realized that the worst that could happen was that they could either say, "No, I'm not single" or "Sorry, I'm not interested."

"Attend the types of events that cater to your niche market. Really put yourself out there and socialize; get to know people and network!"

Offer value to your community. You can request to be a guest speaker at an event or community center, or offer some sort of promotion, like a one-month free membership, to the people attending a specific event that targets your niche market. By offering something unique, you gain attention and are able to get the names and contact information of attendees of the event. This gives you the opportunity to grow your database of potential clients and matches. It also helps in establishing yourself in the community and gets your name out there.

The Next Step: Marketing

While continuing to network at night, during office hours I would approach the media. There is no better advertisement for your company than getting your name out there through press articles. I used the Internet to research gay cable channels and publications. I then composed a simple letter that I could send to magazines, freelance writers, and radio shows on a moment's notice in the event one of these outlets seemed like an appropriate one for me to pitch a story to. I sent everyone letters, and realized that for every thirty letters that went out, I would receive only a couple of responses.

I soon realized that I needed a hook to make the media interested in doing a story on my company, so I began planning and advertising a unique event. Sticking to my niche, I made contact with a celebrity in the gay community and advertised the event as "win a date with such and such celebrity." Fliers were distributed, and ads were placed in gay magazines—this drew a large crowd of 100 or more single gay men that I was able to network with. Plus, because the event was unique, it attracted media.

Whenever I had an up and coming event, I would send out my letters, and no matter what, I made sure to be prepared for an interview with anyone who expressed interest.

You can also try to barter for press. There are plenty of single editors in small newspapers that are open to running a story about you—if you can find them a date! They can then write about your service with a first hand experience.

Working the room

I made my rounds, asking each guest to fill out a card giving their name, e-mail address, and phone number. Each card was then placed into a raffle. As promised, the winner went on a date with the guest celebrity, and I gained a hundred new potential clients. The guests were given the option of releasing their information to Club Elite for future invites, newsletters, and updates. Only those guests who checked the "yes" box were added to my database.

After e-mailing and/or calling everyone in my new network contact list, I invited those who were interested to come to my office and fill out a profile with me. The profiles would then go into either my client folder or my match's folder.

During the profile/interview process, I quickly learned how important it was to take extensive notes. I also found it helpful to include a photo with each profile so I could remember what the client/match looked like.

Enlisting the help of friends

Advertising is very expensive—the most expensive aspect of the business. So, a cost-effective way to get my company's name out there without paying for formal advertisements was to distribute fliers at major events and fundraisers within my niche market. I was able to get my friends to "volunteer" their time to help me with the distribution of fliers. Advertising, although either time consuming or expensive, is imperative if you want clients to come to you instead of having to personally recruit every client yourself.

Learning as you go

I have found over the past four years that you can do cartwheels to get potential clients interested in your service and you can do your biggest sales pitch, but potential clients will not sign if they are not ready to commit to making their love life a priority. You have to except that and let them walk away. I have had several people walk away and then later contact me when they were ready to commit to finding a partner.

As a matchmaker, it helps to look at the areas in which you excel. My strengths lie in my networking and socializing skills. I'm great at getting our name out there, inviting potential clients, in and then sitting down with them and really getting to know them. I make them feel comfortable, and if they're ready, I'm there to help them.

> *"It's like with any business when you are first starting out—you've got to get yourself out there. You have to go to a lot of events. Meet as many people as possible; try to find out which people in that particular community are influential. Schmooze!"*

Matchmakers' Tales

8

Elaine Schmelkin, a traditional matchmaker

Elaine Schmelkin is a traditional matchmaker in every sense of the word. She has never charged a client for her services, yet she seems to be a successful matchmaker. Mrs. Schmelkin has been making matches for over twenty-two years now, and has seen forty-five matches develop into happy marriages. For Mrs. Schmelkin, matchmaking isn't a career; it's a calling.

It began with PUNCH (Parents with UNmarried CHildren), a group created by Mrs. Schmelkin and three of her friends in 1988. The group was designed to bring together young Jewish singles. Mrs. Schmelkin and her friends began throwing parties for their single children and others within their age range. PUNCH hoped that from these parties connections would be made. If after attending three parties, the young single had made no connection, he or she was then invited to interview with Mrs. Schmelkin.

PUNCH nominated Mrs. Schmelkin for the position of interviewer because she was known among the Jewish community as being very friendly and easy to talk to. Each single was invited into Mrs.

Schmelkin's home where they were then asked the following questions: What do you like in a guy/gal? What do you like to do? What are your likes/dislikes? Where do you see yourself five years from now? She developed a complete roster of detailed questions she would ask everyone that came through her door.

All of Mrs. Schmelkin's notes reside in her little black composition books. After the interviewing process, Mrs. Schmelkin would work to find a match. An interviewee could leave her home with the name and phone number of a match that very same day or wait months. After just a short while, Mrs. Schmelkin had many people calling her for an interview—cousins, brothers, friends—everyone was linked to her in some way, and she quickly was linked to a large network of Jewish singles.

With Mrs. Schmelkin's outstanding success rate, the demand for personal interviews quickly outnumbered the demand for PUNCH's house parties. Mrs. Schmelkin's matchmaking skills quickly grabbed the media's attention, and Jewish organizations began asking her to lecture or host events for them. With her sudden popularity and the onslaught of Jewish singles seeking her service, Mrs. Schmelkin began to realize how extremely lucrative a profession in matchmaking could be.

She spoke with her husband about turning her natural ability into a paying career, but he was adamantly opposed. He explained to her that if she truly wanted to match young singles, it should be for a reason other than financial gain—that reason being mitzvah. Mitzvah is a Hebrew word meaning to earn good deeds.

With good deeds in mind, Mrs. Schmelkin continued matchmaking. She conducted interviews from her home in the evenings, sometimes meeting with three clients at a time. She never had to look for people because they always managed to find her. Wedding season was always a popular time for singles to enlist her services, as the answer to "How did you two meet?" was most often answered with "Mrs. Schmelkin introduced us!"

When asked why Mrs. Schmelkin feels she's been so successful, she explains that by eliminating payment, the pressure is off—both for herself and the client. Her motto: "If it works, it works. If it doesn't, it doesn't." The people that come to Mrs. Schmelkin aren't in any rush, because they're looking for love; and they understand that to find true love, it takes time. It was never her objective to send clients on date after date to find the right match. She made her suggestions (usually three or less) and that was that.

Over the years, Mrs. Schmelkin has brought together hundreds upon hundreds of people. She remains close with many of the people she's helped over the years, but considers five of those couples "family." One man that she matched had lost his parents, so when it came time, Mrs. Schmelkin and her husband threw his engagement party at their house. And at his wedding, it was Mrs. Schmelkin who gave him away.

Although she is no longer matching at the volume she was in years past, Mrs. Schmelkin continues to make matches from her home, using her little black composition books. She's currently working to fill number ten.

In Her Own Words

What is one of your most interesting matchmaking stories?

True and cute story: I had a gentleman come to my house. We had coffee and cake (I try to make everyone as comfortable as possible during an interview). I'm talking to him; I'm looking at him, and I say, "You know, I think that I have the most perfect girl for you. Everything that you want—she has."

So I give him her name and he just looks at me and starts to laugh. So I ask him, "What's so funny?"

And he says, "That's my ex-wife!"

What advice do you have for future matchmakers?

If you have empathy for these people, and if you don't want to waste anyone's time, you absolutely must conduct a personal, face-to-face interview. You have to know where these people are coming from if you want to match them successfully.

People come to me because they know who I am; they know that I really do have their best interest at heart.

The Certified Matchmakers

The Matchmaking Institute is the only school in the United States to certify matchmakers. Over the next few pages, you will meet some of the school's most successful graduates—from New York City to Singapore.

Charlee Brotherton

Charlee is a matchmaker and the owner of Brotherton & Associates Introductions, Inc., in Tulsa, Oklahoma.

She has been in the matchmaking business for over seven years. She acquired the Singles Station Dating Co. in January 2000 and has expanded the service to include six offices. She personally matches clients in addition to managing the introductions of thousands of singles through her business. When she was first introduced to the matchmaking/dating service concept, she loved the idea. Being a certified public accountant, she has a quantitative, logical thought process. For her it made perfect sense to take an organized approach to meet the person you would spend the rest of your life with. Most singles employ a haphazard approach to meeting other singles. They spend more time thinking about the features on a new car than they do about the attributes that they are looking for in a lifelong mate. Picking the right mate is the most important decision you will ever make.

Why did you decide to become a matchmaker?

I actually became a matchmaker by chance. I come from a family of entrepreneurs and wanted to own my own business. I answered an ad for a service business for sale—a business that was over twenty-years old and was "fun to operate and very lucrative." That was the Singles Station, which was started in 1979. It is one of the oldest matchmaking services in the United States. However, becoming certified by the Matchmaking Institute was the best thing I ever did. I was surprised how much I learned. I truly feel I am at the top of the field of matchmakers because of my training through the Institute and my business approach to helping my clients find a mate.

How did you get started?

When I first acquired the Singles Station, I basically operated the business and utilized staff matchmakers. I had too many clients to work one-on-one with all of them. Then I started receiving requests from VIP clients who wanted to work directly with me. I began taking on clients personally and networking with other matchmakers. That is when I learned about the Matchmaking Institute. The Matchmaking

Certification helped take my personal matchmaking business to the next level. Now I operate a separate matchmaking company, Brotherton & Associates Introductions, Inc.

In your opinion, what makes a good match?

I don't look for a "good match." I want a "great match." A "great match" is when you have not only two people with similar interests but also have two people with core values that are in line with one another. The personality profile is a wonderful tool to use for identifying core values and making matches. I think life experiences also play a role in matchmaking. Knowing all about your clients—not only where they are today, but where they came from—helps in putting together a great match. You also must recognize life goals. Two people need to be heading down similar paths with similar goals to ultimately make a life together.

What is one of your most interesting matchmaking stories?

There are so many great stories. I will never forget seeing the first baby born from one of my unions. I realized at that time that the baby would never had been born without my help. My biggest joys have been when I introduced a family, not only a husband and wife. There are many children that need a mom or dad and so many times we have made that happen.

Violet Lim

Violet Lim studied law at the University of Manchester and also holds a masters degree in industrial relations from the London School of Economics.

Violet's former career in international finance left her personally unsatisfied, so she and her husband, Jamie Lee, decided to forfeit their stable incomes to start their own business in the dating industry. Violet and her husband met while he was working towards a degree in Accounting and finance. The couple's first date was over lunch—lunch being the underlying theme of their business, Lunch Actually.

In 2004, Violet became the first Asian to become certified by the Matchmaking Institute™. In April of that same year, Lunch Actually Singapore opened. The second office, in Kuala Lumpur, Malaysia, came along a year and a half later. The Singapore office serves over one thousand members while the Kuala Lumpur office currently has over 150 members.

Why did you decide to become a matchmaker?

I thought the idea for "lunch dating" would be greatly appealing to busy professionals in Asia who don't have the time to find love for themselves. After observing both friends and colleagues struggle to find the time for dating, I created Lunch Actually to solve the problem. My clients and matches first go through the interview process with me, after which I send them out on lunch dates. Everyone has time for lunch!

I have always been a people-person, and I feel that when it comes to making love connections, I'm a natural. When the idea of matchmaking came along, I pounced on the chance to combine my passion for helping people with my knowledge of business relations.

How did you get started?

We secured our initial pool of clients by e-mailing friends and family. We explained what it was that we were doing and they in turn told their friends. We also started an advertising campaign to create brand awareness in our market.

In your opinion, what makes a good match?

I think it is very important for potential matches to share common values.

Of course it is always great when their specific profiles match, i.e., interests and hobbies. However, these preferences and interests are on a much more superficial level and will most likely change over time. For example, if "Amy" and "Bob" both believe that the family should always come first, their chances for a lasting relationship are higher than if they were matched together based on their love for golf.

What is one of your most interesting matchmaking stories?

"Lorraine" was in her late 20s, and a very successful lawyer. We were trying to send her out on her third match with "Matthew." Matthew is in the entertainment business—an unconventional career choice in Asia. Despite the fact that Matthew was both successful and well educated, Lorraine couldn't see past his occupation.

It took us some time to convince her to go on the date, and eventually she gave in, considering it would only be an hour of her time.

They went on their first date . . . and both Matthew and Lorraine were extremely taken with one another. Before we knew it, they had both called to put their membership on hold. And then, we heard they were picking out an engagement ring. One year later, on the exact day that we sent them out to lunch, they were married. And we were invited!

Scott A. and Pamela Stowell

Scott A. and Pamela Stowell became certified matchmakers in 2005. Together, they serve singe adults, over the age of 21, in the central New York region. They also throw singles mixers.

Why did you decide to become a matchmaker?

We recognized that when it comes to dating, there are very few options for singles in central New York. The dating world has changed so much over the years, and we were uncomfortable with the idea that online dating services were supposed to be the answer. So instead of talking about it, we decided to do something about it! We knew that face-to-face matchmaking would be the best way to help singles find their "special someone."

Our strong marriage and friendship has given us the inspiration to help others. We are both very compassionate individuals with great instincts for understanding people. We always put our clients first, and are ecstatic when they call to thank us for introducing them to a great person. We know we're doing the right thing because we're making a difference and having a blast!

How did you get started?

Thanks to successful networking, we made the front page in the Syracuse newspaper's business section within the first week of opening our company. And our local television station provided live coverage of our matchmaking endeavors.

In the beginning, we worked to build our database. After thirty days, we had enough people to start matching.

We recommend gaining a handle on the industry and your business before working with friends and family.

In your opinion, what makes a good match?

The more a potential match has in common, i.e., the better their values are aligned, and the more their personalities click, the more likely it is that a second date will follow. However, if the couple lacks any sort of physical attraction to one another or there is no "chemistry" between them, one of the parties will ultimately lose interest.

What is one of your most interesting matchmaking stories?

We ask our clients for feedback after each date. It's always great when we hear from both sides, "I've found 'the one.'" After only a year as matchmakers, we have already created three long-term relationships.

Julie Ferman

Julie Ferman became a certified matchmaker in 2006. She founded her personal matchmaking service, Cupid's Coach, in 2000 to dignify and simplify the love search process for selective, relationship-minded professionals. Before Cupid's Coach, Julie and her husband owned and operated two Great Expectations centers throughout the 90s, later selling them to launch Cupid's Coach. Together they have brought together over 1,000 couples.

Why did you decide to become a matchmaker?

I know what it feels like to be that great girl with lots to offer and a sincere desire for partnership, who just can't seem to find the right partner, the right fit. I understand that the more "desirable" a person is the more selective he or she will naturally be—I enjoy specializing in people who are accomplished, professional, attractive—people who have it all, who are highly selective, and who want and need to be very private in their search for the ideal partner. Simplifying and short-cutting the dating process and enriching lives along the way, that's what I love doing every day of my life.

How did you get started?

I was destined to become a matchmaker . . . I married the man who sold me my dating service membership in 1990. We ran two successful video dating services for ten years, later selling those companies, and then I lauched Cupid's Coach in 2000.

In your opinion, what makes a good match?

When two people respect and admire each other, when they share a few passions, when their core values are in alignment, when they're truly comfortable together, when it feels like "home" being in each other's company, and when there is a mutual attraction and spark— well, that's a great match. And if they both have the commitment to working through challenges together, growing both personally and as a couple, that's a union destined for greatness.

What is one of your most interesting matchmaking stories?

I love the surprises—my client Susan was impressed with Jack when she met him, but . . . wasn't really attracted. He didn't fit her mental picture of what her man would look like. But smart man that he is, Jack pursued her intently, as he was crazy about her. He tailored the first, second, and third dates to her passions in life (wine tasting, the ballet, a dinner party at his home with fascinating friends) and by date number three she was hooked. They are the happiest married couple I know. I love helping my clients see that Prince Charming just may show up on an unfamiliar horse . . .

Your Matchmaking Questions Answered

9

The following answers are provided by Rob Anderson of Club Elite.

1. What if I'm interested in my client? Is it appropriate to date him/her?

It is imperative that you keep your personal life separate from your professional service. As a single person, it is difficult to attend social mixers and events to look for dates for your clients and not yourself. But you must create boundaries if you want to maintain a professional reputation. It's a small world, and an even smaller world when you're dealing with a niche market.

2. Does the matchmaking process differ when you're matching homosexuals as opposed to heterosexuals?

At the end of the day, we're all just human beings. The same rules and emotions apply. I know a heterosexual female matchmaker who matches lesbian women. It has gained her a lot of media attention because it is an interesting concept, but it all boils down to the same matchmaking formula, helping people find love.

3. What do you do if someone comes to you as a potential client and you know you won't have any appropriate matches for him/her?

I once had a seventy-five-year-old client who had recently lost his partner of thirty-five years. I told him that I didn't feel I had anyone in my database who would make an appropriate match. I told him that I would look around for him, and once I felt I had five to six potential matches for him, I'd give him a call. He could then see the profiles of men I had found, and we could go from there. Honesty and integrity are very important in this business.

4. How much should I charge and for what length of time?

At Club Elite, we charge $1,500 for a three-month membership (in 2006); in the contract we agree to provide an unlimited number of dates ranging anywhere between one and six dates a month. However, when I first started, we offered six-month and yearly contracts. Of course, we charged accordingly, but I found it works better on a three-month basis. If you sign a long-term contract with a difficult client—and you will acquire some—you're stuck with that person for a long time. In our opinion, three months is the way to go for two reasons:

a) If you're experiencing difficulties with a client, it's only for three months. At the end of this period, you are contractually free of them.

b) A three-month contract is far less intimidating than a six-month or yearly. A potential client will be much more willing to try your services for three months. It is then up to you to make those three months wortwhile. Ideally, you will find a match for them within that three months or they, genuinely pleased with your database, will renew their contract.

5. Why do you only charge your clients and not your matches?

Club Elite provides a personalized search. This means that not only do I select potential matches from my database, but I also attend events and social functions to broaden my search. For example, I might be at a charity event when I see the perfect match for "Jerry." I approach the potential match, first asking him if he's single. If he replies, "yes," I explain that I am a matchmaker, and briefly describe the client I have in mind. The potential match may or may not choose to accept the date free of charge.

Matches are not charged because I do not work for them directly. If a match from my database decides he had a good experience with my client, he may then decide he wants me to search for him. Only then does he become a paying client.

6. When networking: I know I shouldn't start a conversation with, "I'm a matchmaker," so how should I begin?

I always begin with small talk. For example, "What are you drinking? . . . Oh really, I've never had one of those . . ." The infamous "What do you do?" question will naturally follow. Ask them about their career first, and they will surely return the question.

Generally speaking, people will be interested in your career because it's unique. Explaining matchmaking to someone who is fairly unfamiliar with the concept is a wonderful conversation piece.

I used to dread networking, but now I can't go anywhere without talking to someone—even when I'm standing in line at Whole Foods.

7. How do you put your clients and matches in contact?

When arranging a date between client and match, I provide each with the basics: first name, occupation, and what they like to do in their spare time. And because I don't use pictures, I give each a detailed physical description. I give my client the match's phone number and together they set a date, whether it be dinner, drinks, etc.

8. What should my client-to-match ratio be, and when first starting out, which should come first?

It is probably safest to say that for every client you should have twelve matches in your database. Whether or not you start with matches or clients is up to you. You will most likely have to hustle more if you take on a client before setting up a database—of course if your database doesn't prove appropriate for your client, you will still be required to hustle.

9. How much money should I reserve for advertising expenses?

Advertising is expensive, with the majority of ads running approximately $1,500 a month. If you cannot afford that, there are ways to get publicity for little more than taking an editor out for lunch or drinks.

10. When a potential client comes in for an interview, should I present him/her with pictures from my "matches" file?

When I first started matchmaking, I presented my potential clients with pictures from my database. I found, however, that this made my job harder. Clients would immediately begin trying to match themselves with the matches they found the most attractive. Most often, the matches they picked out for themselves were all wrong.

They may want a Brad Pitt-looking guy, but the one who looks like Brad is looking for something completely different than the client in front of you. It's not a good idea to get them excited at the faces that they can't have. Your clients can get that disappointment on their own—with you they are looking for success. I find the best way to do that is match the personality and basic looks the person has told me they seek, without showing nameless faces that may be unattainable.

Part III

Step-by-Step Tips for Starting Your Matchmaking Business

Starting Your
Matchmaking Business
10

So you've read the book! But now what? Use the next few pages as a step-by-step guideline for starting your very own matchmaking business. We've summarized the pages of this book, so that during your startup process, you can refer to our "Now What?" outlines to help you along your way.

I. Categorizing Your Company

Taking Care of Business

Before you put together a database, before you choose your first client, and well before you provide your first match, with paper and pen in hand, you must answer, as a business owner:

- Who will be your target audience?
- What will your company offer?
- Where will you be conducting business?
- When will you be conducting business?
- And how?

Your business plan will answer each of these questions in full detail so that someone reading it for the first time will have a clear understanding of what your company is all about.

1. Writing Your Business Plan

Your business plan may never be finalized because you will revise and update your objectives regularly. Don't be intimidated by that blank piece of paper—it's just a rough draft. Remember, nothing is set in stone. Answer the following questions first.

- What types of services will your business offer?
    Face-to-face matchmaking?
    Special event planning?
- Who do you want to reach?
    Specify the age range of your potential clients
    Spell out your niche market
- How many clients will you take on at a time?
- How much do you plan on charging clients?

2. Deciding on Your Business Structure

You need to decide which type of business structure is appropriate.

- Will you enlist the help of external investors? If so, you may want to be incorporated.
- If your company will remain privately owned by you (or you and a partner or partners, you may want to obtain an LLC classification.

As you think about which business structure is best for you, consider your skill set. Are you prepared to handle every aspect of the business from marketing to matching, bookkeeping to networking? If you know that marketing might be a challenge for you, can you think of someone more business-minded with whom you might like to part-ner? While a matchmaking business can definitely be operated by one person alone, it doesn't have to be. Sometimes a balanced partnership is more successful than a one-man or one-woman show.

> It's best to discuss business structure with both a lawyer and accountant, since your classification will be used for tax purposes.

3. Writing Your Pitch

Your pitch describes what it is you and your business will strive to do. With your detailed, organized, and formal business plan complete, it's time to create an enticing description of your company. Make it fun and original yet simple enough that the average person clearly under-stands your business objectives. This pitch is one or two sentences at most.

Use your pitch for everything: business cards, website, advertisements, and press releases. It will serve and enhance your identity as a match-maker. Be aware that creating your pitch will be extremely difficult. It will take weeks of revising. You'll want to come up with a few differ-ent pitches and solicit your friends' opinions on each.

- Is my pitch clear and concise?
- Is the pitch fun and inviting?
- Does the pitch leave any unanswered questions?

4. Choosing Your Name and Tagline

Your name and tagline—much like your pitch—should be original, catchy, descriptive, and self-explanatory. The name of your business will define who you are, what you do, and should separate you from your competitors. A tagline works as a reinforcement of your company

95

name. This tagline can act as both a catchphrase and your business motto. Your name and tagline will work together—one informing the other. Both should be capable of standing alone, but together work as perfect complements. Example: It's Just Lunch's tagline is "Dating for busy professionals."

Recommendation: Throughout your career as a business owner, issues will inevitably arise that will require a professional's attention. For example, you will probably want to hire a professional designer to create your website and business cards. It will also behoove you to have an Intellectual Property (IP) Lawyer and a Certified Public Accountant (CPA) on hand for legality and accounting concerns. You might also choose to hire a Webmaster to update your site from time to time. Use other professionals' talents on a project-to-project basis by hiring them as independent contractors.

Important considerations when choosing your name:

• It's not a good idea to include your personal name in your company name. For example, Sharon's Savvy Singles' Events may be catchy and descriptive, but what if you decide to sell the company? Or what if you want to bring in a partner or outside investors? Consider instead, Savvy Singles' Events—better not to get too personal in your company name.

• Establish a DBA, doing-business-as name, to respect your client's desire for confidentiality. Because most people want their dating life to remain personal and confidential, have credit card charges and/or checks made out to a DBA, such as LM Consulting, instead of your company name, LoveMatch. Your clients will appreciate their ability to remain discrete, while at the same time giving you the option to expand your services to include image or personal coaching, event planning, etc.—all under the consulting umbrella.

5. Obtaining a Trademark

Although applying for a trademark is not necessary, a registered trademark provides your business with higher protection and possibly increased value.

- Domain Name

  Using the Internet, perform a search to see which site, if any, comes up when you type in your chosen company name. Is your name already being used as a .com? If so, you might want to slightly revise your name so that you can use your name as your URL address.

- Trademark Check and Application

  Once you've looked into the availability of your domain name, go to www.uspto.gov. To narrow down your search, the website will ask for your service class. You should enter numbers 41 and 45: entertainment and dating. Type in your chosen name. Do any similar names come up? If so, do the companies with your name also offer the same type of services? Depending on the degree of similarity in name and service, decide if it's worth it to apply for a trademark. When dealing with name similarities, it might be helpful to hire an attorney to better assess your chances at gaining an R label. It will cost you about $350 per class to apply for your tradmark registration—besides any other legal fees. After filing your application, you will have to wait approximately a year before your registration goes through.

II. Creating Your Company

A. Providing Points of Contact

Whether you'll be working from home or plan on using a separate office space, your business will need its very own address, phone line, website, and e-mail account. And don't forget the importance of business cards!

1. Physical Address

If you will be working from a home office, using your home address for your business address is perfectly acceptable. The only thing to avoid when setting up your business address is a post office box address. P.O. boxes tend to look less professional than physical addresses.

2. Business Phone Line

In order to keep a defined line between your personal and professional life, you must set-up a separate phone line for your business. A landline with voice-mail is a good start, but you'll probably want to set-up a cellular account as well. Recommendation: Save your clients money by setting up a toll-free phone number. Each time your toll-free number is called, your account will be billed, not theirs.

3. Website

In the beginning, perfecting your website shouldn't be your number one priority. It is important, however, to set-up at least one page of your website before you can consider yourself open for business. Websites are no longer an option for business owners—they're a necessity. A website is the easiest and fastest way to give your business credibility.

4. Business Cards

A logo or simple design should be created to accompany your name and tagline. This design will become uniform for any and all documents you use, including: invoices, contracts, profiles, web pages, business letters, press materials, and your business cards.

Because networking will be your number one marketing tool, a well-designed business card is imperative to your career. Put thought into each aspect of its design: paper, color, font, logo, and shape. Consider your target market: Will a formal, more traditional business card be most appropriate, or will a unique, eye-catching design work best? If utilized correctly, your business cards will pay for themselves—they're worth the investment.

B. Accounting

Before your business can start making money, you will have to open a bank account to house your earnings. And you'll probably want to set-up a method for accepting credit cards. Research your options so that you can achieve both without paying extraordinary fees.

1. Bank Account

When opening an account, try to find a bank with minimal fees. Often times banks will offer discounts for new business owners.

2. Credit Cards

Although the ability to accept credit cards is not necessary for your business, the option to do so will be appreciated by your clients. When first starting out, PayPal might be your best bet. Anyone is eligible to sign-up for PayPal, but when you use this method your client will be paying you indirectly. Their money will first go to PayPal, which after taking a small commission, will be paid to you. If you want to accept credit cards, you may check and compare different fees at charge.com.

C. Recordkeeping

From the moment you start planning your business, you will need to start a filing system. Absolutely anything that involves money spent or estimated future expenses must be recorded and saved: receipts, tax documents, bank forms, applications, and every official document ever signed by you. For safety precautions, it would be wise to make two copies of each and have two separate folders—one for your own personal records and the other for your accountant. When tax-time rolls around, the extra time you spent maintaining your financial records will prove worthwhile.

III. Covering Your Company

When applying for liability coverage for your business, you should first obtain basic business coverage. Once you have the basic package, apply for professional liability insurance to cover your specific services.

A. Business Coverage

Similar to homeowner's insurance, liability coverage will protect your business's assets. You don't want to lose everything you've worked so hard to create on the off chance there's a fire, flood, or burglary at your office.

B. Professional Liability Coverage

Protect yourself from your clients. You will want each client and each match to sign a release form waiving your responsibility. In the event that someone becomes injured, etc., these forms will protect you from being sued. You may want to search for sample waivers online and then revise them to meet your specific needs.

You should always have a lawyer look over all waiver release forms and contractual agreements before they are given to any clients or matches.

IV. Building Your Database

You need to figure out your niche market in order to know who to target when building your database.

Example: Let's say you've decided your niche market will be women over forty; you will now need to figure out how to create a database of pre-screened men in that particular age range. How do you do this?

A. Immediate Connections

Ask around. Ask everyone you know, and then ask everyone they know: Friends, family, co-workers—they all have the potential to help you grow your database.

B. Research

Find the places and events your potential database might frequent. Check your local listings, magazines, community and online re-sources—singles' events are perfect, but any event that you feel caters to your particular niche will work. Go to these events. Remember: You should be networking at least two nights a week.

C. Making Contact

Start introducing yourself to anyone you feel you might be able to incorporate into your database of eligible matches: "I'm a matchmaker and I'd like to invite you to a pre-screening. I can then start introducing you to some amazing women/men at absolutely no cost to you." The majority of people you ask will be flattered and gladly accept a free membership. It will probably serve your business best if you offer your matches free membership—at least in the beginning.

1. Interviewing Your Matches

Before bringing in a potential match, you must first decide what you will be asking them, what sort of contract they will be signing, and where you will be interviewing them.

a. Your Sales Pitch

Will they be paying? Should they sign a contract? Will you be running a background check? You need to answer these questions for yourself before ever meeting with a match or client. Never meet with clients/matches without knowing exactly what your business is offering.

b. Picking a Place

Choose both a time frame and location in which your potential clients and matches will be able to meet you. Evenings? Lunch? Will they be coming to your office? Will you be going to theirs? Make sure your availability matches theirs—you want to make it as easy for them as possible.

c. Being Prepared

You will have paperwork to go over, forms to fill out, contracts and releases for them to sign, so make sure you present them in an organized fashion. Be very clear with them on the ways in which your business differs from the competition. And be prepared to answer any questions they may have: How will you, as a matchmaker, prove to be successful in matching them? What are you providing and at what price? All forms should explicitly state your terms and conditions.

The great thing about creating a free database is that if you're personable, a good interviewer, and you make them feel comfortable, the free matches in your database may want to hire you so that you can specifically search for them.

V. Securing Your First Client

Whether you're having trouble finding your first client, or you already have a potential client in mind, repeat the steps listed above that you deem applicable. Once you've signed your first client, make sure you give them the best service possible.

A. Defining Your Services

As a matchmaker, your business revolves around a sensitive issue. People tend to be vulnerable when it comes to personal relationships, and matters of the heart, so it is your job to make your clients feel comfortable.

1. Honesty

Your client has to trust you; this means trusting your tastes, your opinions, and your ability to help them. You must be completely honest with them from the beginning, meaning that if you think they might be a difficult person to match, you must tell them. If you're worried you don't have enough matches in your database to suit their needs, explain to them why it might take you longer to send them out on a date.

2. Keeping in Touch

After you've met with your client and their contract has been signed, it is your job to keep in contact with them. They should never have to call you, because you're always one step in front of them. Don't make them call you three times before you get back to them. You must make yourself available to your clients. For example, once a client has gone on his or her date, you should wait no longer than two to three days before placing a follow-up call. And stay on top of your matches! Don't make your client call you for a date.

VI. Staying Organized

Keep detailed records of all your clients and matches. Take notes when talking to your clients and their matches after each date, so it is fresh in your mind.

A. Create a Filing System

Online or on paper—you need to be able to quickly reference past dates and feedback from each date. This is particularly important if problems arise with your client. For example, if clients very much enjoyed their match and the match doesn't like them, they may, in hindsight say that that match was terrible, because they feel rejected. If you have a record of dating feedback you can refer to that with your clients and let them know that at the time, they really enjoyed the match and maybe because it was not a shared attraction it made them feel bad about the date.

B. Accurate Records

Review each client's progress by referring back to the detailed dating feedback file you've created. This is indispensable for date coaching.

This also helps track matching choices and helps you make matching decisions for future matches more effectively.

C. Personal Folders

Each client, as well as each member of your database, should have his or her own file complete with contract, questionnaire, notes, etc. Each personal folder you create should clearly state that specific contract's start and end dates. It will also be helpful for you to include each person's picture, whether it's for your personal use or you plan to show your other matches/clients. Provide a section for feedback and take notes in this section each time you give a follow-up call. Make sure to note in each folder with whom they've gone out with so as to not repeat matches.

VII. Making a Match

When making a match between your client and a potential match, you should first match the client's age and physical preferences. Once you've honed in on physical compatibilities, the next step will be finding matches whose relationship goals and personal values comply with your client's.

A. Using Your Database

You should always try to create matches using your database first. If you run out of potential matches in your database, you will then have to go out and find matches.

1. Flipping Through Your Folders

As soon as you take on a new client, go to your database of personal folders and begin weeding through your options. Start by eliminating the

matches that do not meet your client's age range. Then remove matches that have the physical qualities you feel your client would consider a
"deal-breaker," i.e., bad teeth, no hair, etc. Now, taking the folders you
have left, try to match your potential matches' values to your client's.

a. Relationship Goals and Values

Is your client looking for marriage? Do he or she someday want to
start a family? Was your client very adamant about his or her religious
practices? Does he or she place significant value on their career? Will
they need someone that feels the same?

b. Hobbies and Special Interests

These are really the last and least important elements to match. Once
you've matched ages and physical preferences, as well as values and be-
liefs, finding shared interests and hobbies can be considered an added
bonus. This doesn't mean that you shouldn't try to find the matches
that share your client's interests—the more they have in common the
better.

Make sure you are able to explain to your client why you have chosen
this particular match for them; you'll be satisfying your job requirements as well as their requirements.

B. Searching Elsewhere

If you've already looked through your database for potential matches,
and you've come up short, it's time to go headhunting. Explain to
you client that finding them a match will take you a bit longer, but
reassure them that you will be proactively and specifically looking for
them.

1. Perusing and Socializing

Similar to networking, you will need to get out of your office and start meeting people. As a matchmaker, you should be attending events at least once a week if you want to continue to grow your database, so kill two birds with one stone: Build your database, but with your current client's needs in mind. Hopefully, by the end of the week, you'll have added five more people to your database, two of which will be for your current client.

Remember: Never give out your client's or your matches' phone numbers or last names. You should always act as the go-between until they both have given consent.

There you have it! Everything you need to know to get started, made easily accessible. These pages can be used throughout your career as a matchmaker. Post them in your office, or better yet—use our example to create your very own outline for success. You now know everything you need to know to become a profitable matchmaker. Now what? Make it happen!

Part IV

Additional Materials

Top Ten Questions That You, as a Matchmaker, Should Be Prepared to Answer

1. How many years have you been in the business?

2. What is your success rate? How do you define success?

3. What is your cost?

4. Do you charge for the initial consultation/interview?

5. How many matches are promised and over what period of time?

6. Will the same person who conducts my initial interview be matchmaking for me?

7. Do you send me out on dates automatically or do I have to call for an introduction?

8. If I don't like a match you have chosen for me, may I decline?

9. May I view a sample contract?

10. How many clients do you have and how do you search for matches?

Sample Questions When Interviewing a Client

- Why are you looking for a matchmaker?

- What would make you a good partner?

- Are you more old-fashioned or modern?
  (You can give examples: man pays, mom raises children vs. pay 50/50 for dinners and nanny for kids.)

- Are you a person with a positive outlook who thinks things will turn out for the best, or do you worry about things that could go wrong?

- Where do you like to shop for clothes? And do you have a favorite designer?

- Do you consider your style to be chic, trendy, elegant, preppy, sexy, classic, casual, sportswear, not fashionable, don't care?

- What do you do on the weekends and in your spare time?

- What are the celebrities you prefer or resemble the most?

- What are the five items you can't live without?

- What do you do for fun?

- What's the last thing you read purely for the pleasure of it, and what did you think of it?

- Who has been the most influential person in your life, and how has this person been an influence?

- What are the top four things your friends would say about you?

- What are the three things for which you are most thankful?

- What is the first thing people notice about you?

- What is the one thing that people don't notice about you right away that you wish they would?

- Describe one thing about yourself that only your best friends know.

- Are you close with your family? How often do you contact them?

How to Get Certified

So you have now read *Matchmaking From Fun to Profit*. What is the next step? Well, if you are truly serious about entering this exciting industry, why not get certified?

The Matchmaking Institute[SM] has created a certification program which is a highly specialized curriculum of classes put together to teach future matchmakers matchmaking skills as well as provide all the tools needed to become a Certified Matchmaker and start a business in the matchmaking industry with credentials.

The Matchmaking Certificate Program is offered in an eleven-class schedule with twenty-two hours of course work. This intensive three-day weekend training includes specialized classes in areas such as:

- screening techniques
- behavioral communication
- interviewing skills
- matching techniques
- dating feedback and role-playing
- techniques in recruiting new clients
- how to start and run your business
- PR and advertising
- client management—and more

The Matchmaking Institute^SM, following a strict code of ethics and standards, has established a program designed to train those who wish to become certified Matchmakers, while providing practical knowledge that will help individuals start or improve a matchmaking business.

When you get trained and certified, you gain knowledge, support, credibility, and a career. All students who have received a Certificate in Matchmaking from the Matchmaking Institute^SM and have opened businesses and enrolled in the Matchmakers Network, which is an association of certified and professional Matchmakers worldwide.

Just a few of the advantages of being part of the network are: You receive "free press." The Matchmaking Institute^SM is regularly featured in national magazines, newspapers, television, so as member of the network you are getting exposure that you may not have gotten otherwise. You may receive potential client referrals. Your photo and bio are listed on the Matchmaking Institute's website for great local and national exposure.

Matchmaking is one of the fastest growing industries and continues to grow in demand and in profitability every year. It is now time to meet the need for matchmakers to be recognized as serious professionals who have been trained and qualified. Nurses are licensed, social workers are certified, teachers are licensed . . . now, thanks to the Matchmaking Institute℠, matchmakers are certified. You too can become a Certified Matchmaker!

Sample Certificate

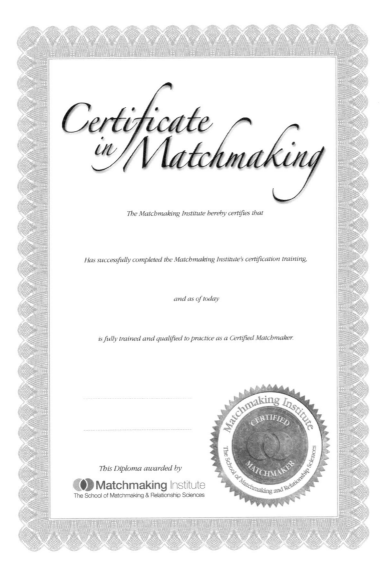

Certificate in Matchmaking

The Matchmaking Institute hereby certifies that

Has successfully completed the Matchmaking Institute's certification training,

and as of today

is fully trained and qualified to practice as a Certified Matchmaker.

This Diploma awarded by

Matchmaking Institute
The School of Matchmaking & Relationship Sciences

Course Outline for Matchmaking Certification^{SM}

Introduction to the Field of Matchmaking

Students will gain an understanding of the role of the matchmaker. The weekend outline and material will be reviewed. Additionally, formal introductions will be made and students will be encouraged to discuss their experiences and career desires in the matchmaking industry with their instructor.

An Overview of the Dating and Matchmaking Industry

Students will gain an understanding of the history and current-day value of the matchmaking industry (singles market, dating industry, and key players in the industry), as well as trends and growth in the market (from offline to online dating, from online dating to matchmaking).

Matchmaking Business Models

Students will learn about different matchmaking business models, including pricing structures and services offered. Existing matchmaking and dating services will be reviewed.

Prescreening Techniques

Students will learn how to prescreen potential clients in person and over the phone. Prescreening forms will be provided and reviewed by the students. Instructor will discuss techniques that optimize strategies for choosing the most desirable clients based on these prescreening forms. Students will role-play their prescreening techniques with each other and feedback will be provided by the instructor and classmates.

Interviewing Techniques and Information Acquisition

Appropriate interviewing skills will be taught in order to gain maximum information efficiently from potential clients for profile development. Profile forms will be handed out and reviewed. Interviewing techniques, providing a comfortable and friendly environment, and privacy for potential clients will be discussed. Instructor will lead a role-playing exercise to demonstrate methods of skillful information acquisition.

Date and Relationship Coaching

Successful dating and relationships techniques will be taught in order to provide clients with the appropriate dating and relationship advice. Students will be provided with the key elements for achieving successful dating and relationship lives. Key information will be given in the following areas: overcoming shyness, isolation and loneliness, becoming a successful listener and speaker, building confidence, and overcoming fear of rejection.

Human Behavioral Communications

Verbal and non-verbal communication skills will be discussed. Students will learn methods to competently comprehend non-verbal body language, be aware of behavioral cues exhibited by clients, and understand verbal tone. In order to better communicate and understand clients, students will be taught to listen to their intuition. Students are encouraged to practice reading verbal tones and body language with their peers and instructor during this session.

Working with Difficult Clients and Maintaining Professional Boundaries

Students will learn to professionally address difficulties with clients. Instructor will offer actual examples that have taken place when working with clients in a matchmaking business. Various solutions and strategies for alleviating client problems will be discussed. Strategies and techniques that facilitate conflict resolution and depersonalization will be taught. These skills will be reviewed and practiced through open discussions and role-playing.

Event Strategy and Conversation

You'll learn how to choose the events you and your clients attend for maximum return on investment of time and money: how to make an indelible first impression, how to work a room gracefully and efficiently, and how to become a master in the art of conversation.

Just Sell, Baby!

Basic sales course for new salespeople or up-and-coming stars. Most salespeople have never received any formal training. As a result, they waste time with trial and error, hoping to hit on the right formula. This class takes the mystery out of your sales process and starts getting results. This program will help students build an effective sales process that will deliver consistent results. These adjustments will have an immediate effect on your bottom line. Topics include: how to open more doors, understanding what you really sell, dealing with different types of people, how to close and when to walk away.

Event Planning and Marketing for Matchmakers

Students will learn how to plan and promote an event. Once we have covered the preplanning, students will learn how to make events successful by creating the right environment using themes and ice breakers. We will conclude with an overview of successful events as case studies.

How to Use the Internet for Your Small Business

Students will learn how to file an application for a trademark, register a new domain name, start or improve their website visibility and ranking, create and use Google ad words, and set-up e-mail rules. The instructor will provide a demonstration of these techniques. Students will also learn how to process credit cards. They will then be able to review and discuss the details concerning the type of matchmaking they want to achieve and the steps they need to take to begin a successful and profitable matchmaking business.

Matchmakers Network and Matchmaking Database

Students will learn about the Matchmaking Network, sharing resources, using the message board, and doing searches in the database. Students will also learn how to set up their own area on the Matchmakers Network™ database and input client information into the confidential database. Benefits of membership including upcoming teleclasses and discounts for members will be discussed.

Public Relations, Networking, and Sales for Matchmakers

Now that you are certified, how do you get your first client? Students will learn the secrets to the successful PR and marketing of a matchmaking business. Learn how to maximize your current network's potential, to take advantage of the many opportunities around you every day. You will learn to expand your network; increase business development with minimum time, effort, and expense; and enhance visibility and credibility. Students will also gain an understanding about the use of press releases and how to garner attention from media.

Registration Coupon
- $100 off! -

With the purchase of this book, you are entitled to a $100 discount when registering for a three-day certification training at the Matchmaking Institute[SM].

Just e-mail us at coupon@matchmakinginstitute.com with your contact information: first and last name, mailing address, e-mail address, and date and place of purchase to receive your discount code within the next two business days.

This coupon is also valid for your relatives, friends, and colleagues.

The Matchmakers Network

The Matchmaking Institute[SM] **has established the very first world-wide Matchmakers Network of Professional and Certified Matchmakers.**

For the first time, matchmakers are able to share resources, support one another, share referrals, and gain national expansion without having to open up offices all over the country.

Many singles contact us daily, either looking to hire a matchmaker or requesting to be posted on our Matchmaker Multiple Listing Service (MMLS), where they are pre-screened and background-checked. This concept is similar to the Real Estate MLS. The real estate industry, as we know it today, has used this idea since the early 1970s and could not survive without it. We feel that using this same concept will re-invent our industry in a totally positive way. This gives each network member great exposure to a pool of potential matches or potential clients.

As a result, you have the support of a network while maintaining the privacy of your business. It's a great concept, and the time has come for us to be recognized as a viable industry!

Some of the many immediate benefits of joining the national network are:

First, it allows matchmakers across the country to pool their resources to facilitate matches on a national scale.

Second, the network helps indvidual matchmakers gain substantial exposure through the enormous amount of press and web traffic that the Institute has been generating, in places such as *Time* magazine, *The Wall Street Journal,* ABC's *20/20,* and *Oprah,* among many others.

On a larger scale, a major goal of the network is to mainstream the matchmaking industry by removing the stigma and mystery historically attached to it. We feel we can accomplish this if business-oriented, forward-thinking matchmakers across the country work together in a way similar to other professional organizations.

The time has come for us to join our forces together as a hard-working professional community!

Contributors

Lisa Clampitt, CSW, is the cofounder and executive director of the Matchmaking Institute^{SM}, a professional matchmaker and a New York State Certified Social Worker for over fifteen years. She was educated at New York University, receiving a BA in dramatic literature, and received her graduate degree, a Master in Social Work, from the University of Michigan. Lisa has many years of experience in individual and couples counseling as well as in relationship and date coaching and has owned her own very successful matchmaking company, VIP Life, for over six years. With this experience and her extensive knowledge of the matchmaking industry under her belt, she went on to create the Matchmaking Institute^{SM} in order to train and certify others, establishing a strict code of ethics in this important industry. Lisa is consistently sought after as a matchmaking and relationship expert and has had extensive international press coverage. Lisa is married and lives in New York City with her husband Frank.

Jerome Chasques is cofounder of the Matchmaking Institute^{SM}. He also runs a publishing company in New York City and has successfully managed four different businesses over the last fourteen years. He holds a Master's degree in business and finance from Institute d'Etudes

Politiques de Paris (Sciences Po) and a Master's degree in business law. The new concept he created in 2002, Dinner in the Dark, has been featured in many publications both nationwide and worldwide. Prior to founding the Matchmaking Institute, Jerome produced educational and cultural programs on CD-ROMs and DVDs in Europe, including the award-winning "The Louvre Museum" title. In 1998, Jerome founded "Mr. Cinema," an entertainment news portal later acquired by Liberty Surf Group, a thensubsidiary of Bernard Arnault's fashion group LVMH. Jerome loves connecting people together and always brings innovative products and concepts to the market. Jerome is married and lives in New York City; he and his wife Nathalie just celebrated their ten-year anniversary.

Rob Anderson is the Director of Club Elite, an exclusive New York City matchmaking service for professional gay men looking for long term relationships. He graduated from the Nash Academy of Animal Arts and worked as a professional dog groomer for fifteen years. An entrepreneur, Rob developed his own business, "Dog's Best Friend," but then switched from pets to people. Rob is one of the first matchmakers certified by the Matchmaking Institute and the only gay certified matchmaker in the world. As a gay man born and raised in NYC, he has seen the first hand struggles that single gay guys go through when searching for that special person. This was motivation to become more involved in his community by bringing romance and the possibility of relationships to the lives of professional gay men. Rob lives with his partner in New York.

Jill Weaver was owner of a large introduction service in Pennsylvania, MatchMaker International, for over eight years. Her franchise was one of the oldest and most respected introduction services in the region. During her eight year directorship, Jill brought over 1,200 singles together and tripled her multi-county client base. Her expertise is derived from a decade of relationship coaching, with a concentration in the areas of single parenting, motherless daughters (founded a local chapter), and domestic violence. Jill and her company have contributed and appeared in numerous periodicals on the art and science of matchmaking. Jill attended Clarion University and the Penn State University in pursuit of her social work/psychology studies.

Steven Sacks is the creator of the Mate Map^{SM} system and noted expert on mate selection. In 2002, he published *The Mate Map: The Right Tool for Choosing the Right Mate*, a book detailing his patented system. Steven is also a dynamic and highly sought-after speaker and relationship coach. He currently teaches a seminar for the Matchmaking Institute^{SM} on relationship sciences using his book and Mate Map system to teach new matchmakers how to select potential matches for their clients. Steve splits his downtime between his hometown of New York City and Durham, North Carolina, with his wife—the first Mate Map success story.

Personal Notes

_____

_____

_____

_____

_____

_____

_____

_____

_____

_____

_____

_____

Feedback

We value the feedback of our readers very highly. Feel free to send your comments, suggestions, questions, or even testimonials to:

Matchmaking Institute[SM]
89 Fifth Avenue, Suite 602
New York, NY 10003
USA

feedback@matchmakinginstitute.com

More About the Matchmaking Institute

The Matchmaking Institute, created in 2003 by Jerome Chasques and Lisa Clampitt, CSW, was established to set a code of ethics and strict quality standards in the matchmaking industry. It is the first institute to offer matchmaking training and certification, introduce singles to Certified Matchmakers[SM], and provide matchmakers with a network of peers and support.

The mainstream success of online dating has opened the door to using a third party to find love and has skyrocketed the popularity of modern-day, one-on-one, personalized matchmaking services. Now more than ever before is it acceptable to use a matchmaker, but with this growth of the matchmaking market comes a greater need for quality control in the industry. So with years of exposure to the pros and cons of the market, our team has collaborated in the creation of a new generation of matchmaking.

www.matchmakinginstitute.com